Grades
4-6

LANGUAGE ARTS

Why practice key curriculum skills using games? Games provide the perfect opportunity for students to engage in active learning, take part in social interactions, and—let's not forget—have fun!

With literacy standards in mind, we designed each game in *Games Galore—Language Arts* to add purpose to students' play. Through hands-on, partner, small-group, and whole-class games, your students will review key literacy concepts as well as foster communication, cooperation, problem-solving, and critical-thinking skills.

Games Galore—Language Arts is also designed to save you time. The comprehensive table of contents conveniently lists each game by skill, so you can quickly find a perfect fit for your curriculum needs. Plus "How to Use This Book" (page 4) will familiarize you with the book's helpful design and easy-to-use contents. Enjoy, and let the games begin!

©2002 by THE EDUCATION CENTER, INC.
All rights reserved.
ISBN #1-56234-486-2

Manufactured in the United States

10 9 8 7 6 5 4 3 2 1

Table of Contents

Spelling & Vocabulary

Reading & Research

How to Use This Book

What makes *Games Galore—Language Arts* as exciting for you as it is for your students? The easy-to-use organization, of course! Each game is designed with the following features:

- **Skill:** Identify the skill in a snap.
- **Number of players:** Quickly note partner, small-group, and whole-class games.
- **Materials:** Round up needed supplies based on this handy reference.
- **Object of the game:** Decide if a game provides the skill practice your students need.
- **Playing the game:** Cleverly written to the student, these directions are printed on a white background so you can easily copy them and place them with the game for student reference.
- **Reproducible page(s):** Find a reproducible—such as a student record sheet, gameboard, or pattern—located on the page following each game description.

Some of the games will contain the following to make preparation or play even easier!

- **Teacher preparation:** If there is advanced preparation needed to set up the game, refer to these step-by-step instructions.
- **Variation:** Extend the life of a game by adjusting the rules, setup, skill, or difficulty.
- **Answer keys:** While many games rely on student knowledge and teacher monitoring, you will find necessary answer keys at the back of the book for handy reference.

Stirring Up Sentence Sense!

Skill: using parts of speech to construct sentences

Number of players: 2

Materials for each player:
- copy of page 6
- lined paper
- pencil
- scissors
- glue

Object of the game:

to earn the most points for creating sentences that use as many parts of speech as possible

Playing the game:

1. Assemble the dice patterns as directed on page 6.
2. To play, each player takes a turn rolling his points die. The person with the highest number goes first.
3. Player 1 begins by rolling his parts of speech die. Next, he writes a word on his paper using that part of speech. Then he rolls the points die and writes that number above his word.
4. Player 2 takes a turn in the same manner.
5. Play continues with each player rolling both the parts of speech die and the points die. With each roll, the player adds words to his paper to create a sentence. (Additional words might be necessary for the sentence to make sense but do not count for points.)
6. Play continues until one player has a complete sentence. That player earns the total points for all the words in his sentence. A new round begins as in Step 2.
7. At the end of 30 minutes, total all the points. The player with more points is declared the winner.

©The Education Center, Inc.

Variation:

Have students play as directed above but construct sentences that are part of an ongoing story.

Directions:

1. Carefully cut out the cube patterns along the outside edges.
2. Place the patterns printed side up on your desk. For each pattern, fold along the uncut solid lines to form a cube. (The words and numbers should be on the outside of the cubes.)
3. Glue the tabs to the inside of the cubes.

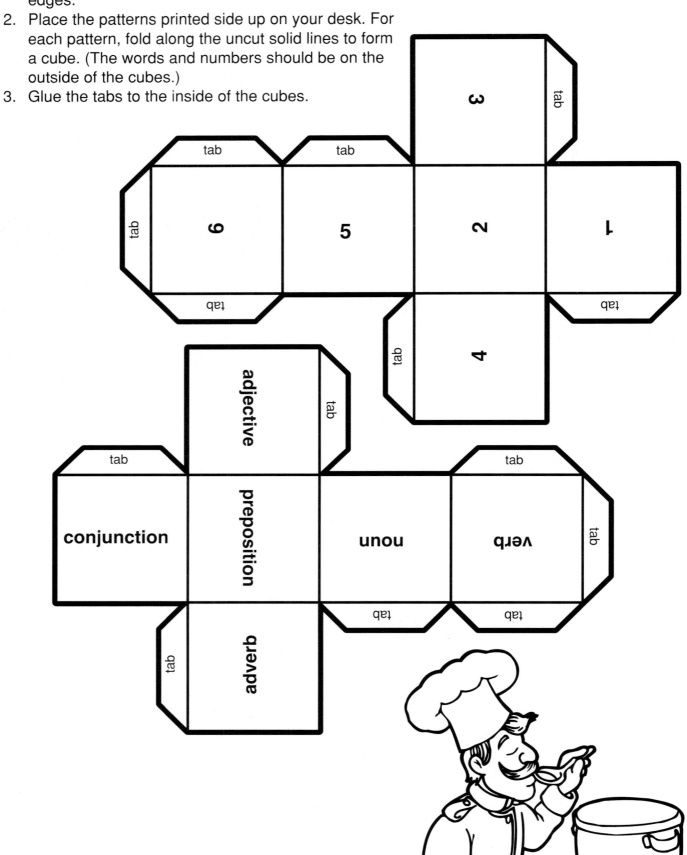

Triple-Scoop Grammar

Skill: using parts of speech

Number of players: 2

Materials for each pair:

- copy of spinner pattern on page 8
- scissors
- paper clip
- pencil
- die
- 6 self-adhesive dots
- marker
- dictionary
- copy of gameboard pattern on page 8 for each student

Object of the game:

to write the player's initials in three consecutive scoops on the gameboard

Playing the game:

1. Make a letter cube by affixing a self-adhesive dot on each side of the die. Then use a marker to label each dot with a different one of the following consonants: *r, s, t, l, n, p.*
2. Follow the directions on page 8 to create a spinner.
3. To play, Player 1 rolls the die and spins the spinner. Then Player 1 thinks of a word that begins with the consonant shown on the die and that is also the part of speech shown on the spinner.
4. Player 2 uses the dictionary to check Player 1's word. If the word is correct, Player 1 writes his initials on the corresponding ice-cream scoop on the gameboard. If Player 1's initials are already on the scoop, he takes another turn. If Player 2's initials are on the scoop, Player 1 loses his turn.
5. Play continues with each player taking a turn rolling the die and spinning the spinner. The first player to have three consecutive scoops with his initials on the gameboard (diagonally, horizontally, or vertically) is the winner.

Directions for making a spinner:

1. Cut out the spinner pattern along the heavy solid line.
2. Place a paper clip in the middle of the spinner.
3. Stand a pencil in the paper clip with one hand and spin the clip with the other hand.

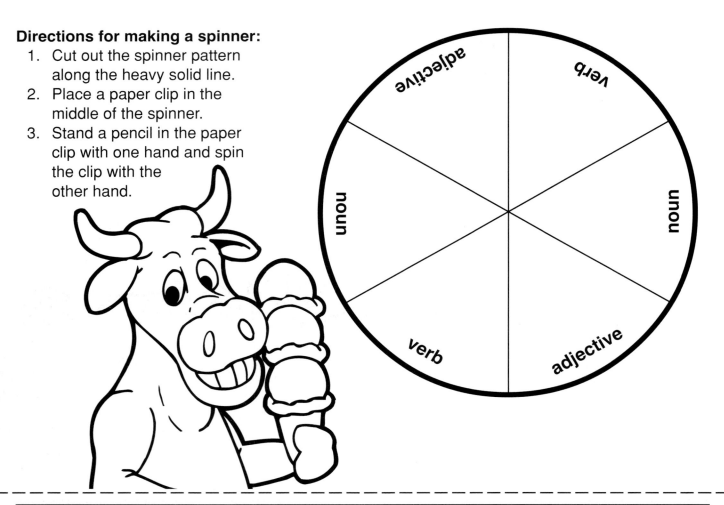

Player 1 _____   Player 2 _____

Triple-Scoop Grammar Gameboard

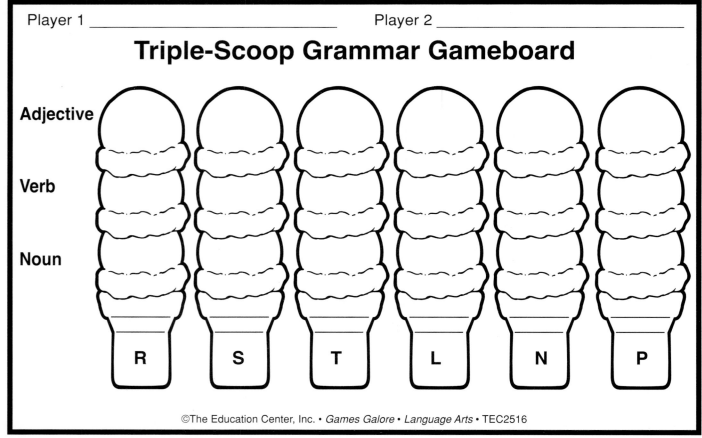

Adjective

Verb

Noun

R   S   T   L   N   P

Initial Possibilities

Skill: identifying and using parts of speech

Number of players: 2–4

Materials:
- 2 construction paper copies of the letter cards on page 10 for every two players
- scissors for each group
- pencil for each player
- lined paper for each player

Object of the game:

to earn the most points by creating sentences with words that begin with the letters on the cards and are used as the part of speech written

Playing the game:

1. Cut the letter cards apart along the solid black lines.
2. Shuffle the cards and deal six cards to each player.
3. To play, Player 1 tries to use all of his letter cards to form a sentence. The words must begin with the letters on the cards. Player 1 writes his sentence on his paper. (Additional words might be necessary for the sentence to make sense but do not count for points.)
4. Player 1's sentence is checked by the other players. Points are calculated using the number at the top of each card. If Player 1 was able to begin a word with the letter indicated and use the part of speech shown at the bottom of the card, the amount of points awarded for that word are doubled.
5. Play continues with each player taking a turn creating a sentence. Six new cards are dealt after each round. A new game begins when there aren't enough cards for a hand. The player with the most points is declared the winner.

Variation:

Add nine wild cards to the deck. Program every three cards with one of the following parts of speech: conjunction, article, or preposition. Write a 6 in the upper left-hand corner of each card to indicate the amount of points each wild card is worth.

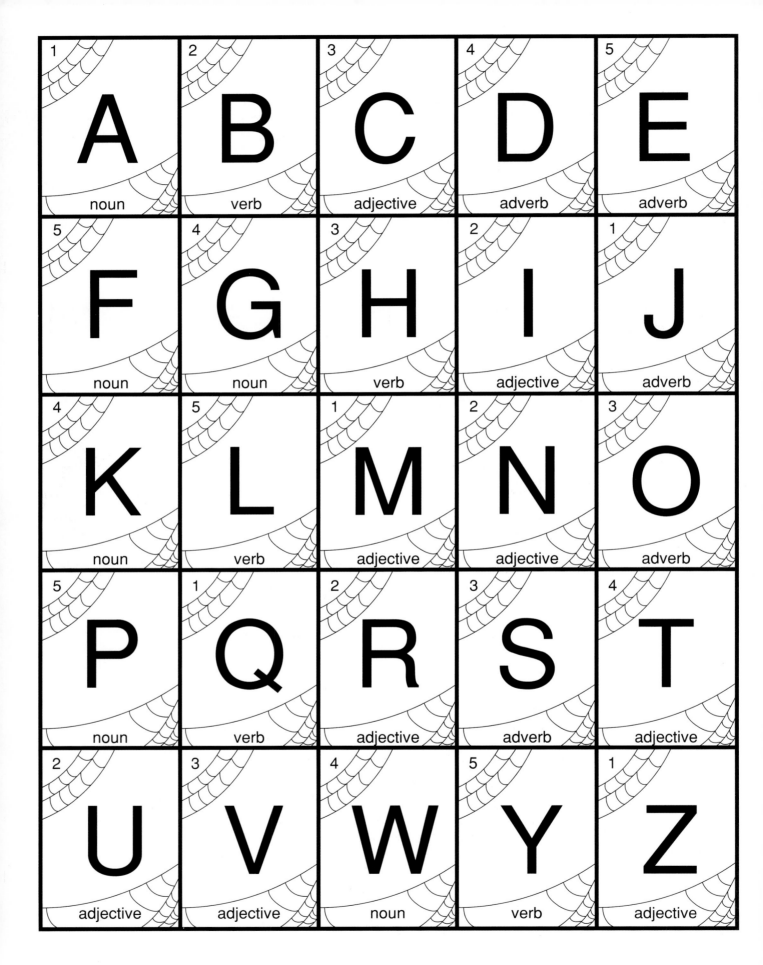

1 A noun	**2** B verb	**3** C adjective	**4** D adverb	**5** E adverb
5 F noun	**4** G noun	**3** H verb	**2** I adjective	**1** J adverb
4 K noun	**5** L verb	**1** M adjective	**2** N adjective	**3** O adverb
5 P noun	**1** Q verb	**2** R adjective	**3** S adverb	**4** T adjective
2 U adjective	**3** V adjective	**4** W noun	**5** Y verb	**1** Z adjective

A Variety of Verbs

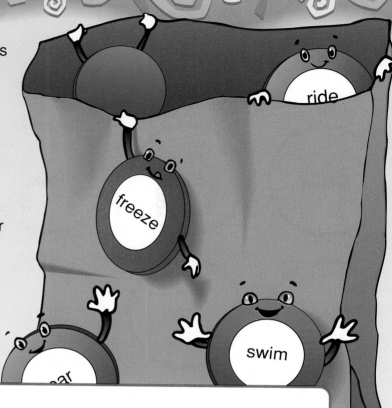

Skill: identifying and using irregular verbs

Number of players: 4

Materials:
- copy of page 12
- 30 bingo chips or other round tokens
- tape
- brown paper lunch bag
- scissors
- die
- dictionary
- lined paper
- pencil

Object of the game:

to correctly identify more past tense and past participle forms of irregular verbs

Playing the game:

1. Cut out the circles on page 12.
2. Loop a piece of tape; then use the tape to attach a circle to a bingo chip. Repeat with remaining circles and chips. Place the chips in a brown paper bag.
3. Player pairs roll the die. The pair with the highest roll is designated as Team 1. Team 1 goes first.
4. To play, a player from Team 1 rolls the die, draws a chip from the bag, and then announces the irregular verb aloud.
5. If the number rolled is even, Team 1 writes the past tense form of the verb on the paper. (For example, if the irregular verb chosen was *rise,* the past tense form would be *rose.*) If the number rolled is odd, the team writes the past participle form of the verb. (For example, if the irregular verb chosen was *rise,* the past participle form would be *risen.*)
6. If the verb form is correct, the team scores the number of points rolled. If the sentence is incorrect, no points are scored. Team 2 may use the dictionary to check Team 1's answer.
7. Play continues with each team taking a turn identifying the correct irregular verb forms. After all of the chips have been used, the team with more points is declared the winner.

Variation:

Divide the class into three teams. Play the game as described above except require teams to use the irregular verb form in a sentence before earning the points rolled.

begin	bite	catch	dive	do
draw	eat	fall	fly	freeze
give	go	hide	know	ride
ring	run	see	shake	sing
speak	steal	swim	swing	take
tear	throw	wake	wear	write

Picture-Proper

Skill: using proper nouns

Number of players: 2

Materials:
- 2 copies of page 14
- die
- stopwatch or watch with a second hand
- pencil
- lined paper for each player
- dictionary for each player

Object of the game:
to earn more points by writing as many proper nouns for each category as possible

Playing the game:

1. To play, Player 1 rolls the die. She then writes as many proper nouns as the number shown on the die under one of the categories on page 14. Player 2 acts as the timekeeper, allowing one minute per category.
2. Player 1 continues rolling the die and writing proper nouns until every category on her paper has been used. If she takes longer than one minute to fill in a category, she marks an X in the category box and continues playing.
3. Then Player 2 plays as described in Steps 1 and 2 while Player 1 acts as the timekeeper.
4. When both players are finished playing, they swap papers and tally each other's score. One point is awarded for each correctly written proper noun. A point is deducted from the final score for each X marked on a player's paper. The player with the higher score is declared the winner.

Variation:

Challenge students to play the game as described above, but to number the words to show alphabetical order.

Picture-Proper

bodies of water	songs	candy bars
presidents	holidays	cars
movies	singers/groups	countries
cities	teams	actors

Handy-Dandy Descriptors

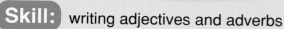

Skill: writing adjectives and adverbs

Number of players: 2

Materials:
- copy of page 16
- pencil
- die
- 6 self-adhesive dots
- marker
- dictionary
- stopwatch or watch with a second hand

Object of the game:
to write more adjectives and adverbs in a designated amount of time

Playing the game:

1. Make an adjective-and-adverb cube by affixing a self-adhesive dot to each side of the die. Then use a marker to label three of the dots "adj." and three "adv."
2. To play, Player 1 rolls the die while Player 2 acts as the timekeeper. (A time limit should be set prior to play.)
3. Player 1 checks the appropriate box and then writes either an adjective or an adverb beginning with the letter *A* in the space provided on page 16. After Player 1 writes a word (or if he cannot think of one), he rolls again and tries to write either an adjective or an adverb on the next line. Player 1 continues playing in this manner until he reaches the last letter line or until time runs out.
4. Player 2 uses a dictionary to check the words listed; then he records Player 1's score.
5. Player 2 takes a turn in the same manner, except Player 2 cannot repeat any of the adjectives or adverbs from Player 1's list. After Player 2 writes his last adjective or adverb, Player 1 records Player 2's score on the line provided.
6. The player with more correctly written adjectives and adverbs is declared the winner.

Handy-Dandy Descriptors

Player 1 _____	Adjective	Adverb	Player 2 _____	Adjective	Adverb
Score _____			Score _____		
A	☐	☐	A	☐	☐
B	☐	☐	B	☐	☐
C	☐	☐	C	☐	☐
D	☐	☐	D	☐	☐
E	☐	☐	E	☐	☐
F	☐	☐	F	☐	☐
G	☐	☐	G	☐	☐
H	☐	☐	H	☐	☐
I	☐	☐	I	☐	☐
J	☐	☐	J	☐	☐
K	☐	☐	K	☐	☐
L	☐	☐	L	☐	☐
M	☐	☐	M	☐	☐
N	☐	☐	N	☐	☐
O	☐	☐	O	☐	☐
P	☐	☐	P	☐	☐
Q	☐	☐	Q	☐	☐
R	☐	☐	R	☐	☐
S	☐	☐	S	☐	☐
T	☐	☐	T	☐	☐
U	☐	☐	U	☐	☐
V or W	☐	☐	V or W	☐	☐
X, Y, or Z	☐	☐	X, Y, or Z	☐	☐

Marathon Modifiers

Skill: using correct modifiers

Number of players: 2

Materials:
- copy of page 18
- scissors
- die
- 2 game pieces
- 2 sheets of lined paper
- 2 pencils

Object of the game:

to "run" more miles by correctly using modifiers in complete sentences

Playing the game:

1. Cut off the race path at the bottom of page 18. Write each player's name on the line provided.
2. To play, players place their game pieces on any space on the gameboard.
3. Player 1 rolls the die and then moves her game piece clockwise to the correct space.
4. Player 1 uses the key in the middle of the gameboard to help her read the space. Then she writes a sentence(s) about the topic using either a superlative or a comparative modifier. Player 2 checks Player 1's sentence(s). One mile is awarded for each correctly written sentence.
5. Player 2 takes a turn in the same manner.
6. Players continue to play. The player who reaches the finish line first is declared the winner.

©The Education Center, Inc.

Variation:

Program 30 index cards each with a different superlative or comparative modifier. Play as directed above, but challenge students to draw a card and use the modifier listed in at least one of her sentences.

Marathon Modifiers

Roll Again	**your town** 4 (C)	**shopping** 1 (S)	Roll Again
your favorite TV show 2 (S)			**your family** 1 (★)
winter 1 (★)			**music** 2 (S)
a book character 2 (C)	**KEY**		**your state** 3 (C)
your school 1 (★)	S = superlative c = Comparative ★ = superlative or comparative		**movies** 2 (★)
swimming 3 (S)	Example: S → shopping → 1 ↑ ↑ ↑ S topic number of sentences to be written		**your teacher** 4 (S)
Roll Again	**summer** 3 (S)	**sports** 2 (★)	Roll Again

©The Education Center, Inc. • Games Galore • Language Arts • TEC2516

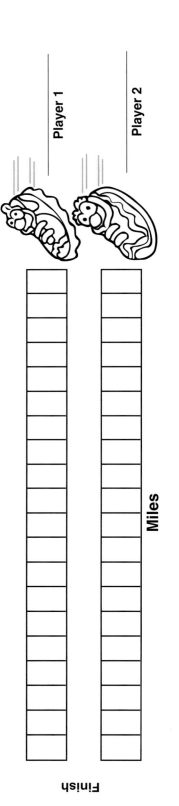

Player 1

Player 2

Miles

Finish

Agreeable Sentences

Skill: identifying subject-verb agreement

Number of players: 2

Materials:
- copy of the cards on page 20
- 20 index cards
- scissors
- glue
- pencil for each player
- lined paper for each player

Object of the game:
to create more sentences by correctly matching a subject card and a verb card

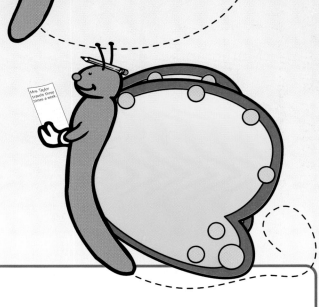

Playing the game:
1. Cut apart the cards on page 20 along the solid black lines. Next, glue each card to the blank side of an index card.
2. Shuffle the cards; then spread them out facedown on a table or desk.
3. To play, Player 1 turns over two cards. If he turns over a subject card and a verb card, he determines whether the cards can be combined to begin a sentence. If they can, he writes the subject and the verb on his paper and adds words to flesh out his sentence. Then he keeps the cards and takes another turn.
4. If Player 1 does not choose a subject card and a verb card or if the two cards cannot be combined to form a sentence, he turns the cards back over, and Player 2 takes a turn.
5. Play continues until all of the cards have been used. The player who writes more sentences is declared the winner.

Tom	The team	My brothers and his friends	Mrs. Taylor
Tanya and her brothers	Parents	My teacher	Sydney
Martin and Keith	The dog	stand	runs
wake	talk	feeds	travels
make	speaks	eats	grows

Building Beginnings

Skill: writing sentences using different beginnings

Number of players: 2–4

Materials:
- copy of page 22
- scissors
- 2 paper clips
- 2 pencils
- lined paper
- stopwatch or watch with a second hand

Object of the game:

to be the first player to earn ten points by constructing sentences

Playing the game:

1. Cut out and assemble the spinners as directed on page 22.
2. To play, Player 1 spins spinner A for a sentence topic. Then he spins spinner B to determine how to begin his sentence.
3. Player 2 acts as the timekeeper, allowing Player 1 one minute to write a complete sentence.
4. Player 1 writes a sentence using the topic and the sentence beginning from spinners A and B.
5. Player 2 calls time at the end of one minute; then Player 1 shares his sentence. A point is awarded if the sentence is written correctly in the time allowed.
6. Play continues with each player in turn acting as the time-keeper and spinning to build sentences. The first player to earn ten points for using the suggested topics and sentence beginnings is declared the winner.

Directions for making a spinner:
1. Cut out the spinner pattern along the heavy solid line.
2. Place a paper clip in the middle of the spinner.
3. Stand a pencil in the paper clip with one hand and spin the clip with the other hand.

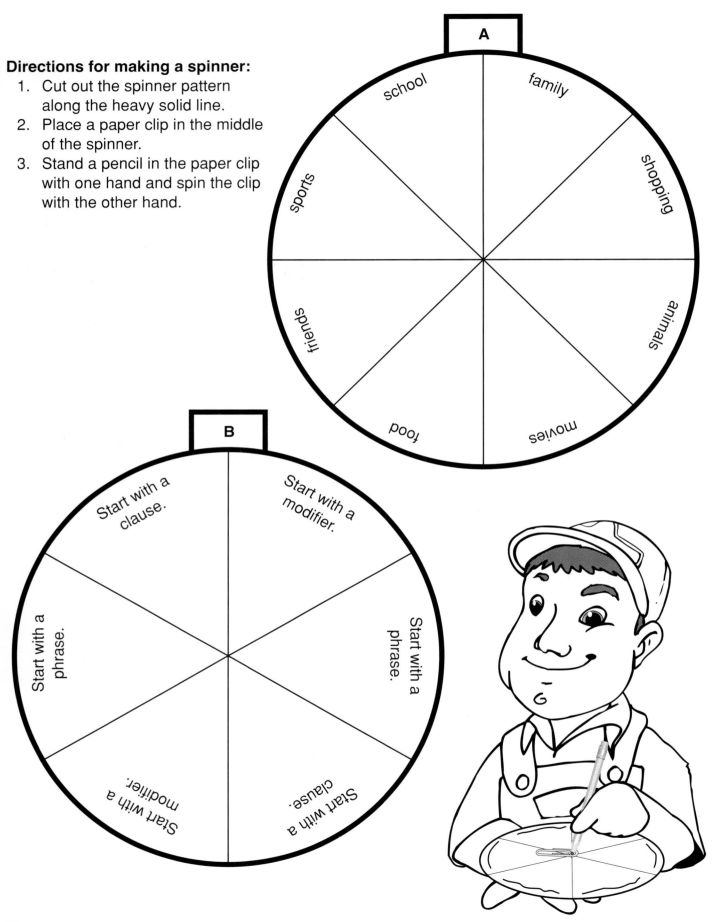

Spinner A segments: family, shopping, animals, movies, food, friends, sports, school

Spinner B segments: Start with a modifier. Start with a phrase. Start with a clause. Start with a modifier. Start with a phrase. Start with a clause.

"Ssss-entences"

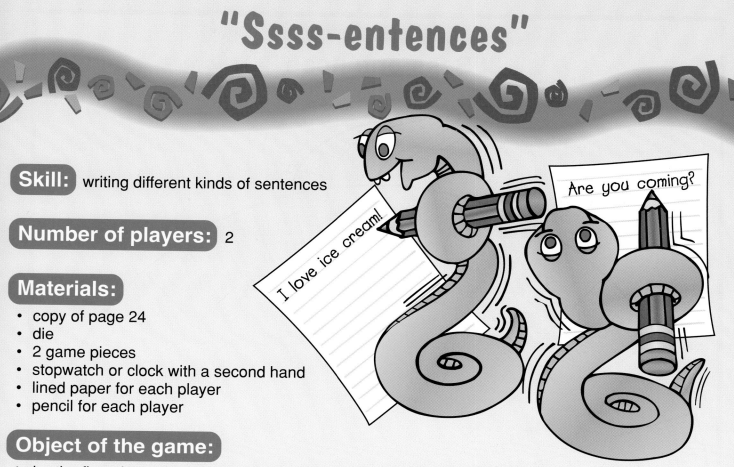

Skill: writing different kinds of sentences

Number of players: 2

Materials:
- copy of page 24
- die
- 2 game pieces
- stopwatch or clock with a second hand
- lined paper for each player
- pencil for each player

Object of the game:

to be the first player to reach the finish space by correctly writing different kinds of sentences

Playing the game:
1. To play, players place the game pieces on the start space on the gameboard.
2. Player 1 rolls the die and then moves her game piece counterclockwise to the indicated space.
3. Player 2 acts as the timekeeper.
4. Player 1 writes either a declarative, imperative, interrogative, or exclamatory sentence on her paper in 30 seconds. When the time is up, Player 2 checks Player 1's sentence for correctness. If the sentence is incorrect, Player 1 returns to her previous spot on the gameboard.
5. Player 2 takes a turn in the same manner.
6. When a player lands on an arrow space, she moves her game piece down to the next level on the gameboard and continues playing.
7. Players continue to play as directed above. The player who reaches the finish space first is declared the winner.

Variation:

For less advanced students, write the symbol for each kind of sentence (period, question mark, exclamation point) on the spaces before reproducing the gameboard.

"Ssss-entences"

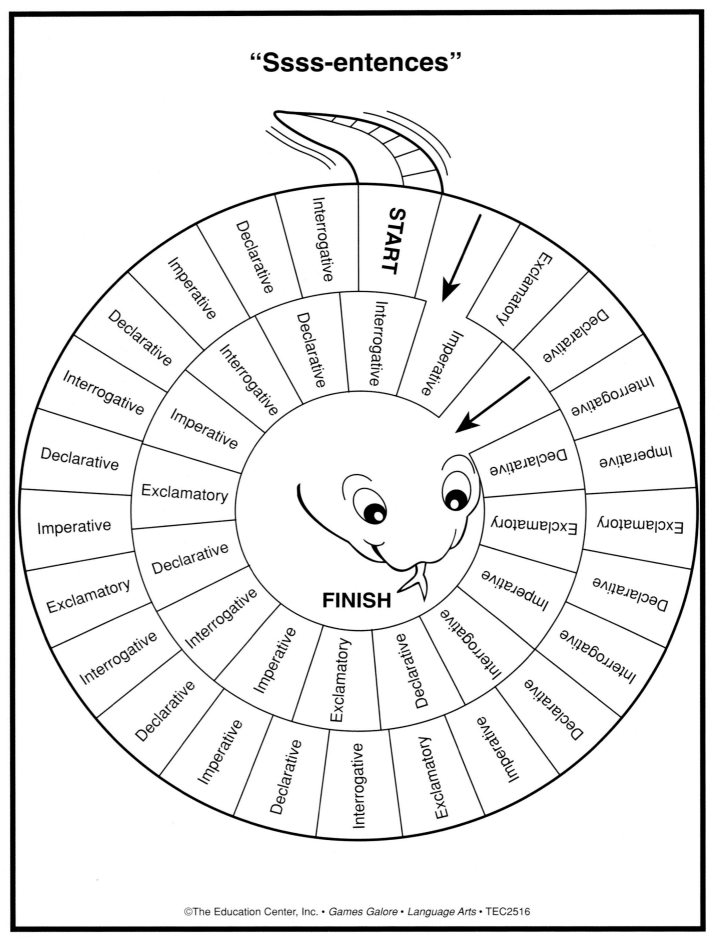

Buzzing About Sentences

Skill: identifying kinds of sentences

Number of players: 2

Materials:
- copy of page 26
- set of 16 prepared index cards (lined)
- stopwatch or clock with a second hand
- lined paper
- pencil

Teacher preparation:

1. Ahead of time, cut each index card in half vertically.
2. Divide the cards into four groups of eight. On the blank side of each card in one group, write a declarative sentence. Likewise, write interrogative, imperative, or exclamatory sentences on the remaining groups of cards.
3. On the lined side of each card, write which type of sentence is displayed, using the abbreviations *D, IN, IM,* or *E.*

Object of the game:

to correctly identify each type of sentence shown on the cards in the designated amount of time

Playing the game:

1. Shuffle the cards so that the sentences are facing up. Do not look at the backs of the cards.
2. Player 1 acts as the timekeeper.
3. Player 2 reads the sentence on the first card and then places the card on the correct spot on the gameboard.
4. Player 2 continues playing in this manner until one minute has passed.
5. Next, Player 2 turns over each pile of cards. Player 1 looks at the back of each card to determine whether the card is in the correct pile. For each correctly placed card, Player 2 receives a point. Player 1 records Player 2's score.
6. Player 1 takes a turn in the same manner.
7. The player who correctly places the larger number of sentences in the designated amount of time is declared the winner.

Variation:

Provide students with the index cards and direct them to make up their own declarative, interrogative, imperative, or exclamatory sentences.

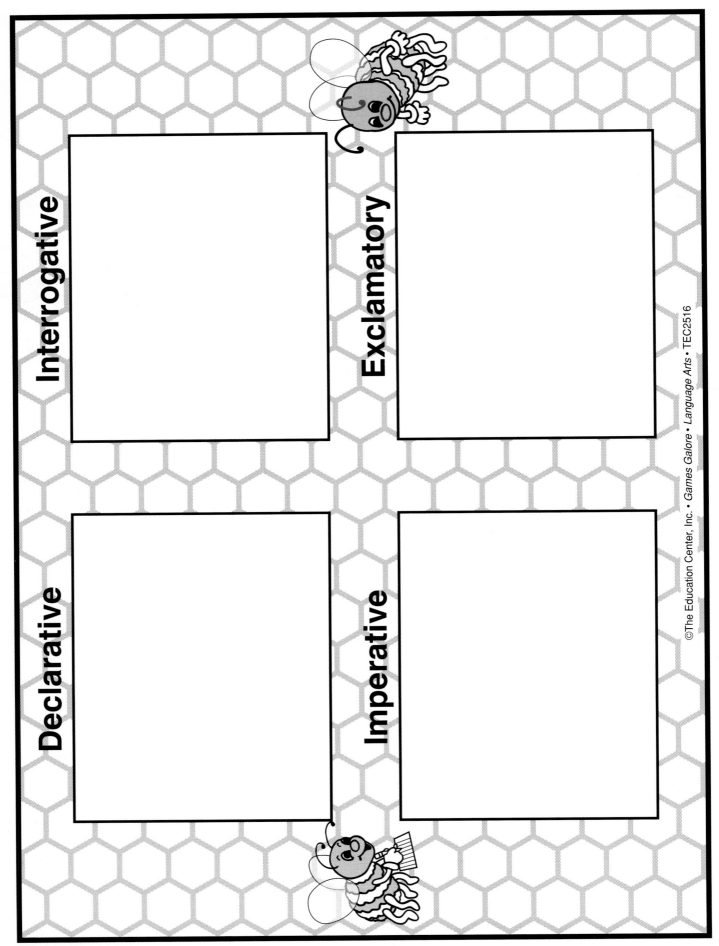

Interrogative

Exclamatory

Declarative

Imperative

Sixth Sense for Sentences

Skill: identifying types of sentences

Number of players: 2–4

Materials:
- copy of the sentence strips on page 28
- die
- paper lunch bag
- lined paper for each player
- pencil for each player
- copy of the answer key on page 95
- white, letter-sized envelope
- scissors

Teacher preparation:

Place the answer key inside the envelope and seal it.

Object of the game:

to collect the most points for correctly identifying simple, compound, and complex sentences

Playing the game:
1. Cut apart the sentence strips on page 28 and place them in the paper bag.
2. Each player numbers her paper from 1 to 20.
3. To play, Player 1 rolls the die, then removes a sentence strip from the bag. The player reads the number and the sentence aloud.
4. Each player determines the type of sentence, then writes either "simple," "compound," or "complex" next to the correct number on her paper. The player also records the number rolled on the die.
5. Play continues with each player, in turn, rolling the die and drawing a sentence strip from the bag.
6. When all of the sentences have been used, Player 1 opens the envelope and reads the answers for each sentence aloud. If a player has correctly identified the sentence, then she is awarded the number of points rolled for that sentence. After totaling all of the points, the player with the highest score wins.

Sixth Sense for Sentences

1. My sister's name is Natasha, and my brother's name is Phillip.

2. Natasha, Phillip, and I recently went to a Mets game, where we were able to sit near the dugout and see players like Mike Piazza, John Franco, and Rick Reed up close.

3. Natasha bought herself popcorn, but I saved my money for a souvenir.

4. When it started to rain, we feared the game might be canceled or delayed.

5. People around us sang songs.

6. The game continued after the rain stopped, and the Mets won!

7. The Mets are my favorite team, but my brother prefers the Yankees.

8. Because he is my favorite player, I hope to meet Benny Agbayani someday.

9. Jay Payton hit the winning run!

10. The crowd was overjoyed, and people cheered wildly.

11. We felt lucky to see such a good game.

12. When he thought he'd forgotten his hat at the stadium, Phillip got nervous.

13. In case he'd forgotten, I reminded him that he had given his hat to me to hold.

14. Phillip was relieved to know his hat wasn't lost.

15. Mom had soup, sandwiches, and salad waiting for us at home.

16. Because we were hungry, we were grateful to see the food waiting.

17. I told Mom all about the rain, and Phillip told her about Jay Payton's hit.

18. Mom was excited for us.

19. We went up to bed.

20. It had been a long day!

Capital Strategy

Skill: using capitalization

Number of players: 2

Materials:
- copy of page 30
- scissors
- glue
- different-colored pencil for each player
- watch with a second hand

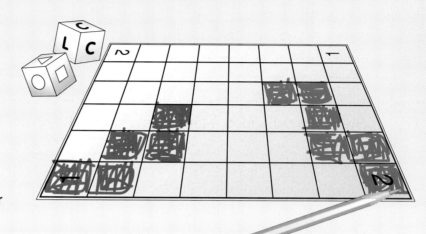

Object of the game:
to be the first player to reach the opposite corner of the gameboard by using correct capitalization with nouns

Playing the game:
1. Cut out and assemble the dice.
2. Each player sits on his side of the gameboard and colors his numbered square. This square then becomes the player's starting point.
3. Player 1 rolls both dice. One die indicates a noun category (person, place, or thing), and the other die tells whether the noun must have a lowercase or capital letter.
4. Player 1 has ten seconds to name a noun that matches the roll of both dice. For example, Player 1 might name the Statue of Liberty for a thing requiring a capital letter.
5. If Player 1 gives a correct answer, he chooses an adjoining square, either horizontally or vertically (not diagonally) and colors it. If his answer is incorrect, he does not color a square and his next turn begins from the same location.
6. Player 2 takes a turn in the same manner.
7. A player may not move to a square that has already been colored. If a player becomes blocked, he loses a turn but may jump over one square on his next turn.
8. The first player to reach the opposite corner of the gameboard wins.

©The Education Center, Inc.

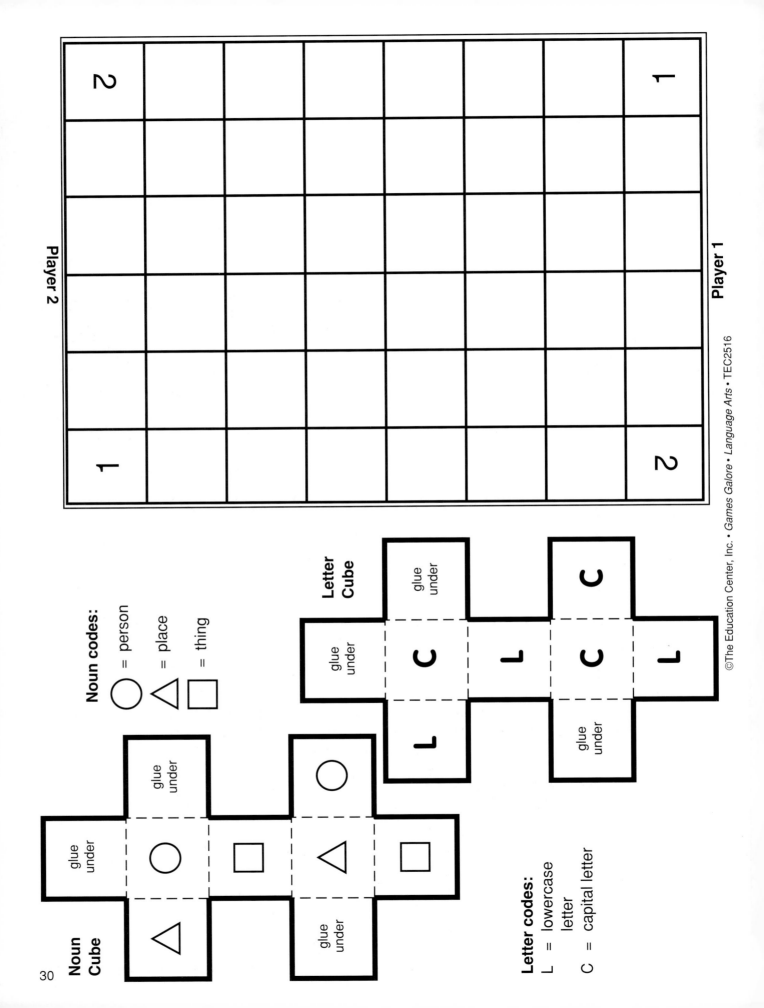

Player 1

Player 2

| | | | | | | | 2 |
| 1 | | | | | | | |

Letter Cube

Letter codes:
- L = lowercase letter
- C = capital letter

Noun Cube

Noun codes:
- ◯ = person
- △ = place
- ☐ = thing

30

Score Four

Skill: capitalization

Number of players: whole class

Materials:
- overhead projector
- overhead transparency
- permanent marker
- wipe-off marker
- copy of page 32
- chalkboard
- chalk
- scissors

Teacher preparation:

1. Prepare an overhead transparency with a permanent four-by-four grid, similar to a tic-tac-toe board.
2. Make a copy of page 32 and cut out the cards. Choose 16 cards to use for the first round.
3. Place the transparency on the overhead projector and a card, facedown, in each space on the grid.
4. Divide students into Team X and Team O.

Object of the game:

to be the first team to score four correct answers in a row on the grid—horizontally, vertically, or diagonally

Playing the game:

1. Player 1 on Team X goes to the overhead and picks up a card from the grid.
2. The player reads aloud the instructions on the card and then writes his response on the chalkboard. A second player from Team X may go to the board and make any necessary corrections.
3. If Team X has written a sentence or list that follows the directions and is capitalized correctly, the teacher puts an X in that space on the grid. If not, the team receives no mark.
4. Team O sends its first player to the overhead to choose a card. Play continues as explained in Steps 2 and 3 above.
5. The first team to score four marks in a row wins the round.
6. If time allows, play a second round. Wipe off the marks on the grid and rearrange the 16 cards, replacing some cards. Allow Team O to go first in the next round.

Write a sentence using any four capitalized words.	Write the title and author of a favorite book.	Write a sentence that contains a two-word place name.	Write a sentence that contains the name of a governmental body or agency.
Write a sentence using a proper adjective.	Write a sentence that contains the name of an organization.	Write a question that contains the name of a holiday.	Write an exclamatory sentence that contains two capitalized words.
Write a sentence that contains the names of two people.	Write a sentence that contains a direct quotation.	List three important historical events.	Write tomorrow's date, including the day of the week and month.
List three important buildings.	Write a sentence that uses the name of a nationality.	Write your address, including the street, city, state, and zip code.	Write a sentence using a person's title and name.
Write a sentence that uses the name of a body of water.	List five brand-name products.	Write the name of a senator or representative.	Write a sentence that contains three two-word proper nouns.
Write a sentence that refers to a person without using a proper noun.	List three specific places you would like to visit.	Write a sentence that uses the name of a foreign language.	Write a question that contains at least five capital letters.

Capital Checkers

Skill: using capitalization

Number of players: 2

Materials:

- copy of page 34
- standard checkerboard
- 12 black checkers
- 12 red checkers
- set of small self-adhesive stickers numbered 1–24
- 24 prepared index cards
- pencil for each player
- paper for each player

Teacher preparation:

1. Randomly place a numbered sticker on one side of each checker.
2. Cut out the sentence strips from page 34. Glue each strip to a separate index card. Then write the corrected sentence on the back of the card.

Object of the game:

to move more checkers to the opposite side of the gameboard by correctly capitalizing sentences

Playing the game:

1. Each player places her checkers sticker side down on the dark squares of the first three rows on her side of the board.
2. Checkers are moved diagonally forward, and players take turns moving their pieces.
3. Before a player can jump an opponent's checker, she must first look at the number on the bottom of the checker she is going to move. The player looks at the corresponding index card and corrects all capitalization mistakes. Her opponent checks her answers by looking on the back of the card. If correct, the player may jump her opponent and capture the checker. If incorrect, the player's checker is captured by the opponent.
4. Play continues until one player has all of her remaining checkers on the opposite side (last two rows) of the checkerboard. The player with more checkers on the board wins the game.

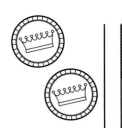

1. I live in greenburg forest, north carolina, on a street called robin lane.

2. "I think spring is my favorite season," said ellen, "but i love snow in january, too."

3. Did you know dave's discount store is having a sale this june?

4. The sea turtle hotel overlooks the atlantic ocean.

5. Last saturday tommy, jeremy, and my brother went to goodby park.

6. His science teacher, mr. markham, also coaches basketball.

7. The spacecraft traveled past mars and jupiter.

8. Does mrs. davis speak french and spanish?

9. On memorial day we went to lake brantley for a picnic.

10. We had cheerios and granola for breakfast.

11. Please take your english and history books home every monday.

12. The tour went through germany, italy, and france.

13. *Mouse of my heart* is a children's book written by margaret wise brown.

14. A russian artist from moscow will show his paintings.

15. On may 14 shelia went to visit her grandmother in denver, colorado.

16. I believe chip arnold is in the sixth grade at fletcher middle school.

17. Our hostess, mrs. walker, served fresh peaches from georgia.

18. We visited fort matanzas in st. augustine, florida, last spring.

19. Next monday carlos will read from a book titled the mystery of the hidden beach.

20. We visited the sears tower in chicago, illinois.

21. The dames point bridge is a suspension bridge on the st. johns river.

22. The barnett bank is downtown on bay street near the museum of science.

23. Has dr. s. t. stanley been to memorial hospital yet today?

24. This book says president reagan acted in the movie *sante fe trail*.

Punctuation Power!

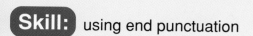**Skill:** using end punctuation

**Number of players:** 3

Materials:

- copy of page 36
- scissors
- glue or tape
- clock or watch with a second hand

**Object of the game:**

to earn points by creating sentences on specific topics with correct end punctuation

Playing the game:

1. Assemble the die pattern on page 36.
2. Cut out the conversation topic cards and place them in a stack facedown.
3. To play, Player 1 draws a card from the stack. The card determines the topic of the players' conversation for the first round of the game.
4. Player 1 rolls the die and has a 15-second time limit to create a sentence on the designated topic, ending with the punctuation shown on the die. Player 3 serves as the timekeeper and judge. A player receives one point for a correct answer.
5. Then Player 2 rolls the die and follows the directions in Step 4. However, now his sentence must continue the conversation that Player 1 has begun.
6. Play continues until a student is unable to create a sentence within 15 seconds, use correct punctuation, or add a sentence that makes sense in the conversation.
7. Play several rounds, each with a new topic. Rotate the duty of timekeeper and judge. The player with the most points is declared the winner.

©The Education Center, Inc.

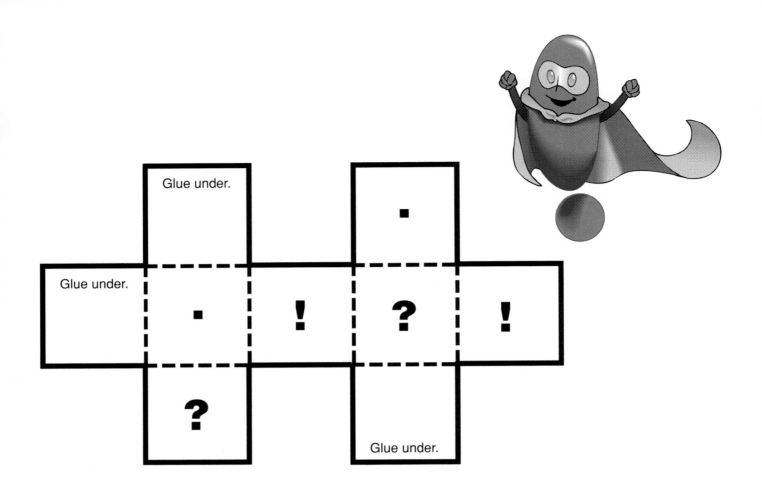

television shows	breakfast foods	soccer	shoes
talking on the telephone	summer vacations	unusual pets	stormy nights
homework	using a computer	cooking	afterschool activities

End Over End

Skill: using end punctuation

Number of players: 2–4

Materials:
- 30 prepared punctuation cards
- 30 prepared sentence cards
- copy of answer key on page 95

Teacher preparation:
1. Cut thirty 3" x 5" index cards in half vertically. On 30 of the half cards write end punctuation marks: periods, question marks, and exclamation marks. Include at least five of each type.
2. Copy and cut apart the sentences on page 38. Glue one onto each remaining half card. Laminate the cards, if desired.

Object of the game:

to get rid of all the punctuation cards in your hand by correctly matching them to sentence cards

Playing the game:
1. Shuffle the punctuation cards and deal five to each player. Place the remainder of the punctuation cards and the deck of sentence cards between the players.
2. To play, Player 1 draws a sentence card, reads it, and decides which type of punctuation is needed at the end of the sentence. If Player 1 is holding a matching punctuation card, she places both down to make a set. If she does not hold a matching punctuation card, she draws another punctuation card. If this card matches, she makes a set. If not, her turn is over.
3. Player 2 takes a turn in the same manner. Players continue to take turns until one player matches all the punctuation cards in her hand. Players may check the answer key for accuracy.

©The Education Center, Inc.

Variation:

Place all cards, both sentence and punctuation cards, facedown in two decks. Players take turns turning over one card from each deck to try to match a sentence with its correct end punctuation. If a match is made, the player picks up the cards and places them to the side. The player who has the most cards when all the possible matches have been made is declared the winner.

The competition is at 10:00	Shall we meet at 8:00	Let's go in a little early
How nervous I am	Get on the bus at the corner	Where shall we sit
I like the back seat the best	How bumpy this street is	Go to check in first
Is this where our team meets	What a huge gym this is	I need to warm up
I think my bag is on the bench	How clumsy I feel	What if I fall during my event
Help me do my stretches	Our team will perform first	Is everyone here
Look at how good that other team is	Let's try to do our best	I will be next
Wish me luck	Did it look as good as I thought	What a relief it is that it's over
I'm sure you'll do just as well	Hang in there	What a super performance that was
Don't you feel great	Make sure you have your medal	What a great day this is

The Dollarama Buyout Store

Skill: using commas

Number of players: 2

Materials:
- copy of page 40
- dice
- envelope
- copy of the answer key on page 95
- different-colored pen for each player

Object of the game:
to earn more money by correctly placing commas in sentences

Teacher preparation:
Place the answer key inside the envelope and seal it.

Playing the game:
1. Player 1 rolls the dice. The number rolled determines the section in which a sentence must be corrected by adding commas. For example, if Player 1 rolls a seven, he correctly adds commas to one of the sentences in section seven.
2. Player 2 takes a turn in the same manner. If a player rolls a number that indicates a section in which both sentences have already been corrected, his turn ends.
3. After all the sentences have been corrected, players may challenge each other. If a player thinks his opponent has made an error, he challenges his opponent by circling an incorrectly placed comma or adding a missed comma with his pen.
4. After all the challenges have been made, players open the answer key envelope, check the sentences, and tally the money earned for each sentence. A player earns one dollar for every comma he correctly adds. For any correct challenge, a player earns one dollar and his opponent loses two dollars. However, if a player incorrectly challenges his opponent, the challenger loses two dollars and his opponent gains none. The player who earns more money to spend at the Dollarama is declared the winner.

©The Education Center, Inc.

Variation:
Have students write the sentences to be used for the game. The skill may change to practice using other punctuation, capitalization, subject and verb agreement, etc.

Player 1 _____   Player 2 _____

The Dollarama Buyout Store

#	Sentence	$ Player 1	$ Player 2
2	Susan bought popcorn, soda a hot dog and chips at the game.		
	Wow! My aunt lives in Calgary too.		
3	Emma when was the last time you saw Jeff?		
	The package contained a yo-yo puzzle cassette tape and book.		
4	Well are you coming to the game?		
	Mr. Sherman is a doctor and he owns his own Internet business.		
5	It was a cold rainy windy night.		
	I think I saw him yesterday Kate.		
6	Mrs. Sherman is a nurse and she has a degree in business.		
	Jerry Kim and Nancy need to take lessons this summer.		
7	Ryan Brendan, and Tara are expert swimmers.		
	"No I think I will stay home."		
8	"Will you leave tomorrow Albert?"		
	My best subjects are reading, Spanish science and history.		
9	I did well in math, science health and reading.		
	We returned to Oakland California on May 26 2001.		
10	My birthday is April 17 1991.		
	Yes and I will take Lena with me Rose.		
11	My pen pal Kendra lives in Calgary Alberta.		
	He drove an old rusty secondhand car to the theater.		
12	We left for Tampa Florida on March 16 2002.		
	I was born on July 3 1990.		
	Total:		

Comma Wall Ball

Skill: using commas

Number of players: 2

Materials:
- copy of page 42
- 2 different-colored ¹/₂" diameter chenille pom-poms
- notebook paper and pencil
- timer or clock with second hand
- language arts textbook
- tape

Object of the game:

to be the first player to earn 50 points by writing phrases or sentences that match the comma rules represented on the gameboard

Playing the game:

1. Fold the top, left, and right borders of the gameboard page to form walls. Tape the corners to make them square. (The walls help prevent the pom-poms from escaping the gameboard.)
2. Player 1 sets her pom-pom on START and uses her finger to gently flick the ball onto the gameboard.
3. If the pom-pom stops on a numbered space, Player 1 finds the corresponding comma rule listed at the bottom of the gameboard. Then she writes an original phrase or sentence that illustrates the rule and correctly places the comma. Player 2 keeps the time, allowing 30 seconds for a response.
4. Player 2 may challenge the answer, using the language arts textbook as a reference. Correct answers earn the number of points indicated on the playing space. Incorrect answers earn no points.
5. If the ball jumps the wall or lands on a section with a circle, the player loses her turn. If the ball lands on a line, the player must play the higher number.
6. The first player to earn 50 points is declared the winner.

Comma Wall Ball

Fold up.

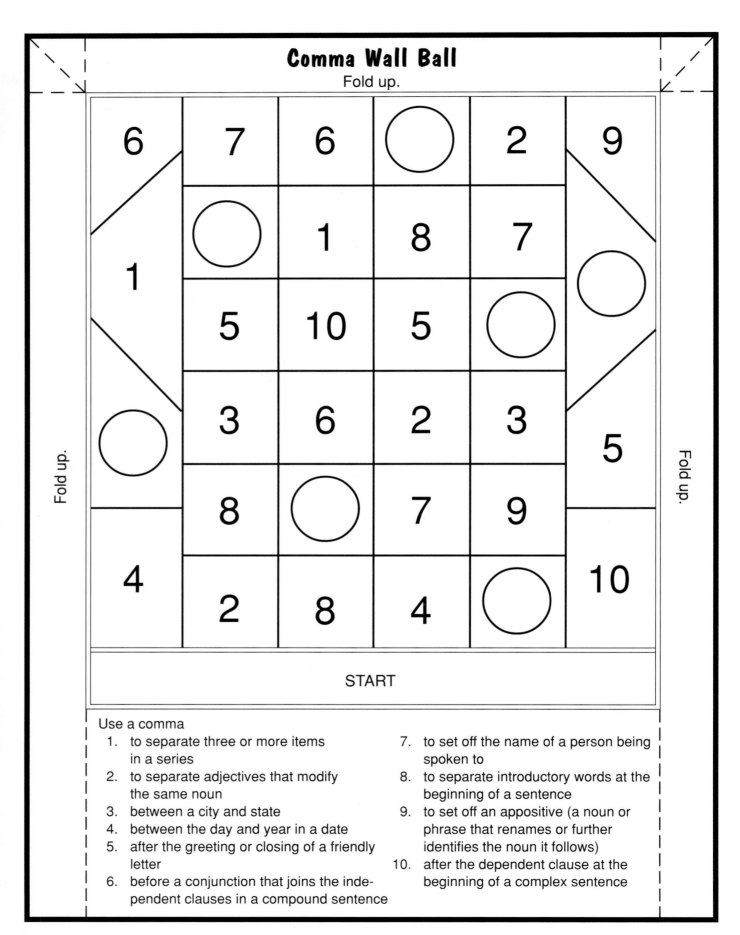

START

Use a comma
1. to separate three or more items in a series
2. to separate adjectives that modify the same noun
3. between a city and state
4. between the day and year in a date
5. after the greeting or closing of a friendly letter
6. before a conjunction that joins the independent clauses in a compound sentence
7. to set off the name of a person being spoken to
8. to separate introductory words at the beginning of a sentence
9. to set off an appositive (a noun or phrase that renames or further identifies the noun it follows)
10. after the dependent clause at the beginning of a complex sentence

You Said It!

Skill: using quotation marks

Number of players: 2

Materials:
- prepared cards from page 44
- die
- paper for each player
- pencil for each player
- watch or clock

Teacher preparation:
1. Cut out the speaker and topic cards from page 44.
2. Cut 21 two-inch squares from two sheets of different-colored construction paper. Glue each category of cards to a different-colored set of paper squares. Assemble the sets into decks.

Object of the game:
to earn the most points by constructing sentences correctly punctuated with quotation marks, commas, and end punctuation

Playing the game:
1. Place the deck of speaker and topic cards facedown between the players.
2. Player 1 draws a card from both the topic and speaker decks. Then he rolls the die to determine the structure of his sentence.
3. Player 1 uses his two cards to construct a sentence that matches the roll of the die. Together the players evaluate the sentence for accuracy. Player 1 earns one point for each correctly used punctuation mark.
4. Player 2 follows the same procedure to construct a sentence and earn points.
5. The player to earn more points at the end of 30 minutes wins the game.

You Said It!

Instructions for sentence structure:

Roll 1 or 2— Write who is speaking at the beginning of the sentence.
　　　　　Example: The teacher said, "Today we will take a test on chapter five."

Roll 3 or 4— Write who is speaking in the middle of the sentence.
　　　　　Example: "Today," said the teacher, "we will take a test on chapter five."

Roll 5 or 6— Write who is speaking at the end of the sentence.
　　　　　Example: "Today we will take a test on chapter five," said the teacher.

©The Education Center, Inc. • *Games Galore* • *Language Arts* • TEC2516

Speakers			Topics		
actor	U.S. president	doctor	bears	movies	clothes
scuba diver	musician	painter	coral reef	cars	election
basketball player	principal	grandmother	rock concert	game	cookies
your best friend	leprechaun	older brother	money	dancing	homework
car salesman	three-year-old	monster	reading	lunch	vacation
artist	father	teacher	slumber party	recess	pizza
fairy godmother	enemy	co-worker	weather	hobby	soccer

You Can Quote Me

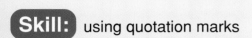

Skill: using quotation marks

Number of players: 3

Materials:
- copy of page 46
- copy of the answer key on page 95
- 2 different-colored game pieces
- die
- small paper bag
- pencil
- scissors

Object of the game:
to score more points by moving around the board and supplying quotation marks and commas in sentences

Playing the game:

1. Cut out the sentence strips on page 46. Deposit the sentence strips in the grab bag.
2. Players 1 and 2 sit side by side and place their game pieces on the central squares. Player 3 serves as the answer checker. Players review the chart to learn the moves on the gameboard.
3. Player 1 draws a sentence strip from the grab bag and reads it aloud. Player 1 then adds quotation marks and commas where needed. The answer checker compares the punctuation to the answer key and announces whether the sentence is correct. If correct, Player 1 earns the number of points shown on the square where his game marker stands. (For his first turn, it will be three.) If incorrect, no points are awarded. Play rotates to Player 2.
4. If Player 1 was incorrect, Player 2 may choose to correct his sentence, or he may draw a new sentence from the grab bag. In either case, Player 2 earns points in the same manner as Player 1.
5. On the next turn, Player 1 rolls the die to determine the direction of his move. Then he may choose to correct an incorrect sentence (if there is one) or a new one from the grab bag. Points are awarded in the same manner as before.
6. If a player's game piece is located on the edge of the gameboard and he cannot move in the direction indicated by the die, he loses his turn. If a player lands on the same square as his opponent, he may move the opponent's token to any other square on the board.
7. Play continues until all the sentence strips have been corrected. The player with more points is declared the winner.

Roll of the Die	Move
●	1 space right ▷
●● (2 diagonal)	1 space ◁ left
●●● (3 diagonal)	1 space forward △
●● ●● (4)	1 space back ▽
●●● ●● (5)	1 space ◁ left and 1 space forward △
●●● ●●● (6)	1 space right ▷ and 1 space back ▽

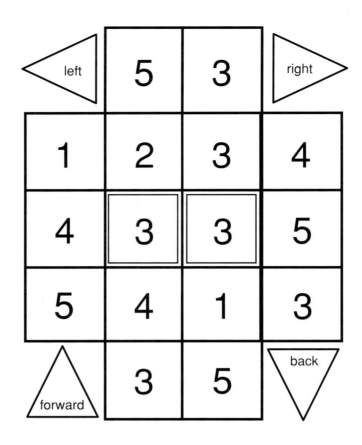

©The Education Center, Inc. • *Games Galore* • *Language Arts* • TEC2516 • Key p. 95

A. We're just trying to keep our heads above water piped the plumbers jointly.

B. It's a dog-eat-dog world! barked the veterinarian impatiently.

C. The firefighter screeched hotly You're just adding fuel to the fire!

D. The actor heartily recited All the world's a stage.

E. If the shoe's too big giggled the clown ridiculously wear it!

F. Too many cooks spoil the broth admitted the chef tastelessly.

G. I'll have ham and cheese on rye ordered the judge decidedly and hold the mustard.

H. If at first you don't succeed instructed the teacher learnedly try, try again.

I. Don't cry babbled the baby wisely over spilled milk.

J. Romeo, Romeo quoted Shakespeare playfully wherefore art thou?

K. The mime thought Silence is golden?

L. Honestly, Princess croaked the frog jumpily there's no reason to kiss me!

M. Let's not split hairs over it! clipped the barber sharply.

N. Shockingly, the electrician snapped We're getting down to the wire!

O. Catch you later panted the runner breathlessly.

P. Put your money guessed the contestant unsurely where your mouth is?

Abbreviation Tessellation

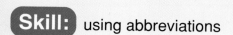

Skill: using abbreviations

Number of players: 2–4

Materials:
- copy of page 48
- scissors
- glue
- game piece for each player
- different-colored pencil for each player
- paper for each player

Object of the game:

to be the first player to earn 200 points by correctly writing abbreviations

Playing the game:

1. Cut out and assemble the die.
2. To play, each player places his game piece in a different circle on the gameboard.
3. Player 1 moves his game piece to any adjoining dot and traces the connecting line with his colored pencil.
4. Player 1 rolls the die and writes an abbreviation from the category shown. If his answer is correct, he earns the number of points indicated on the point key for the shape he is on. Incorrect answers earn no points.
5. Players 2, 3, and 4 follow the same process in turn. Abbreviations may not be repeated.
6. Once a connecting line has been traced, it cannot be used by any other player. A player may land on the same space as an opponent, sending the opponent back to his home circle.
7. The first player to earn 200 points wins the game.

Abbreviation Tessellation

Point Key

Shape	Points
◇	25
○	20
⬡	15
▢	10

Cube template (foldout):

- Glue under.
- Glue under.
- measurement
- title used with a name
- month
- a street address
- state
- day of the week
- Glue under.

Spellbound

Skill: identifying correct and incorrect spellings

Number of players: 3–5

Materials:
- copy of page 50
- game piece for each player
- die
- copy of the answer key on page 95

Object of the game:

to be the first player to make his way to the finish line by recognizing misspelled words and correctly spelling them

Playing the game:

1. Assign one player the job of checking answers. Each of the other players places his game piece on START. Players roll the die and the player with the highest number begins the game.
2. To play, Player 1 rolls the die and moves forward that number of spaces. Then he reads the line that matches the number he rolled.
3. If the line tells Player 1 to do something, such as go back three spaces, the player follows those directions. If the line gives a spelling word, Player 1 must tell if the word is spelled correctly or incorrectly. If the word is incorrect, Player 1 must give the correct spelling.
4. The checker checks the answer with the answer key. If Player 1 is correct, he remains on that space. If he is incorrect, he returns back to the square from which he began his turn.
5. Each player takes turns following the same process. Play continues until one player reaches FINISH with an exact roll of the die.

Variation:

Rather than use a checker, have players take turns looking up spellings in the dictionary.

Spellbound

START

A. 1. friend

B. 1. alot
2. studying

C. 1. humor
2. thier
3. storys

D. 1. auther
2. loaves
3. Roll again.
4. neighbor

E. 1. instead
2. choosen
3. broke
4. Go back 1 space.
5. geting

F. 1. Wednsday
2. piece
3. Switch places with the leader.
4. clothes
5. comeing
6. Go back to Start.

G. 1. Move ahead 1 space.
2. governer
3. finaly
4. happier
5. doctor
6. fourty

H. 1. boxs
2. sugar
3. answer
4. Trade places with any opponent.
5. weight
6. childern

I. 1. disappear
2. truely
3. Saterday
4. continue
5. fiveteen
6. Go back 3 spaces.

J. 1. family
2. ninty
3. already
4. either
5. Lose your next turn.
6. exsept

K. 1. Roll again.
2. wolfs
3. believe
4. keys
5. guest
6. forrest

L. 1. seperate
2. cried
3. Febuary
4. receive
5. Lose your next turn.
6. discribe

M. 1. address
2. decision
3. becuase
4. vegtable
5. certain
6. allways

N. 1. column
2. droping
3. group
4. cheif
5. Go back 2 spaces.
6. necessary

O. 1. arguement
2. favorite
3. easier
4. discuss
5. library
6. Trade places with the player farthest behind you.

P. 1. knowlege
2. excited
3. choclate
4. calender
5. scissors
6. hopeing

Q. 1. definite
2. gaurd
3. imagine
4. colege
5. almost
6. dosen't

R. 1. monkeys
2. Teusday
3. attendence
4. Go back 3 spaces.
5. commitee
6. hunderd

S. 1. begining
2. weird
3. busness
4. familir
5. laugh
6. niece

T. 1. recess
2. goverment
3. Go back 1 space.
4. specail
5. squirrel
6. misspell

U. 1. eight
2. leafs
3. Move ahead to FINISH!
4. aweful
5. Go back 5 spaces.
6. cinnamon

V. 1. usualy
2. enough
3. dictionary
4. feild
5. cocoa
6. Lose your next turn.

W. 1. arithmetic
2. amateur
3. nuisance
4. fasten
5. bisciut
6. similar

FINISH

Spelling Duel

Skill: using conventional spelling

Number of players: 3

Materials:
- copy of page 52
- 2 decks of playing cards
- 20 beans or bingo markers
- list of 20 spelling words
- pencil

Object of the game:

to earn more points by correctly spelling words aloud

Playing the game:

1. Players 1 and 2 each take a shuffled deck of cards and ten bingo markers. Player 3 acts as the caller.
2. Players 1 and 2 sit facing each other. Each player places one card face up between them. The player whose card has the higher value (jacks = 11, queens = 12, kings = 13, and aces = 14) places a marker on any number on the gameboard.
3. The caller reads the spelling word from the list that corresponds to the chosen number.
4. If the player spells the word correctly, she earns the number of points indicated on both played cards and she keeps both cards. If the word is misspelled, no points are earned, and the cards remain on the table for the next round. (The marker remains on the number so that the spelling word is not called again.)
5. If players lay down cards that are equal, each plays another card. All cards are picked up by the player who spells the next correct word, and their point value is added to that player's score.
6. Play continues until all 20 spelling words have been used. At that time, the player with more points wins the game.

Variation:

Provide a list of 20 challenge words in addition to the regular spelling list. Players may choose to spell a challenge word and earn double points.

Player 1 _____   Player 2 _____

Spelling Duel

1 2 3 4 5 6 7 8 9 10

11 12 13 14 15 16 17 18 19 20

Spelling Joust Champion

Player 2 — Points

Player 1 — Points

Think and Link

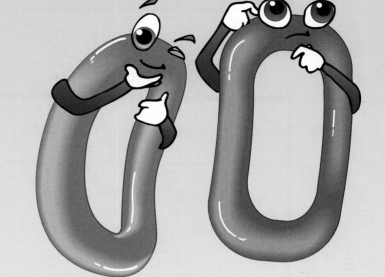

Skill: identifying conventional use of spelling and vowel patterns

Number of players: 2

Materials:
- copy of page 54
- die
- 2 game pieces
- 30 bingo chips or other small counters (15 each of 2 different colors)
- lined paper for each player
- pencil for each player

Object of the game:

to collect more points for recognizing similar spelling and vowel patterns

Playing the game:

1. Determine which color counters each player will use.
2. Player 1 places her game piece on any space on the gameboard, rolls the die, and then moves the game piece that number of spaces in any one direction.
3. Player 1 follows the directions on the key and covers all of the suitable words on the gameboard with her counters. Player 2 awards Player 1 a point for each correctly covered word.
4. Player 2 begins his turn by determining whether Player 1 has overlooked any words on the gameboard. If so, Player 2 can place a counter on each overlooked word and receive two points per word.
5. Player 1 removes her counters and game piece from the board. Player 2 removes any of his counters and then places his game piece anywhere on the board, rolls the die, and moves that number of spaces. Once on the correct space, he follows the directions on the key and is awarded points as in Step 3.
6. Play continues in this manner for 20 minutes. When time is up, the player with the higher number of points is declared the winner.

Player 1 _____ Player 2 _____

Think and Link

(fear)	g<u>ow</u>n	(punch)	bea<u>ch</u>	cl<u>ear</u>	<u>s</u>end	(late)	(night)
beyo<u>nd</u>	b<u>oo</u>k	<u>wh</u>en	el<u>e</u>phant	<u>j</u>ersey	[flower]	fou<u>nd</u>	[power]
b<u>ou</u>nd	[garbage]	perce<u>nt</u>	cr<u>ow</u>d	[gallon]	(plate)	(crook)	r<u>i</u>nd
(fright)	(bright)	(hear)	fl<u>igh</u>t	(pile)	[sight]	m<u>i</u>nd	lun<u>ch</u>
f<u>ee</u>l	h<u>a</u>te	(bend)	[appoint]	whatev<u>er</u>	[cedar]	<u>bl</u>end	(find)
ab<u>ove</u>	c<u>e</u>nt	bou<u>gh</u>t	cl<u>ea</u>r	kn<u>ow</u>	h<u>igh</u>	or<u>ph</u>an	<u>gl</u>ad
w<u>ai</u>t	(file)	<u>wh</u>ile	(tent)	wou<u>nd</u>	[nephew]	(trait)	<u>br</u>eeze
<u>cl</u>ever	s<u>ou</u>nd	<u>kn</u>eel	[fate]	tro<u>ph</u>y	bl<u>i</u>nd	<u>gl</u>ove	[allow]

Puzzle It Out

Skill: using prefixes, suffixes, and root words to make words

Number of players: 2

Materials:
- 2 copies of page 56
- 2 pencils
- stopwatch
- scissors

Object of the game:

to earn the most points by forming words using prefixes, suffixes, and root words

Playing the game:
1. Each player cuts out his puzzle cards on page 56 and places them faceup on the playing surface.
2. One player sets the stopwatch for three minutes.
3. Players race to form either two-part words (prefix and root word or root word and suffix) or three-part words (prefix, root word, and suffix) with their cards, using each card only once. Each player writes his words on his score sheet, being careful to spell each word correctly.
4. When time is up, players swap papers and then tally each other's score. Correctly written two-part words are worth two points and three-part words are worth three points.
5. After each player's points are tallied, the player with the higher score wins.

©The Education Center, Inc.

Variation:

Have each player choose one suffix or prefix card. Place the root word cards faceup on the playing surface. Challenge each player to write words that combine his suffix or prefix and the root words shown. After a set amount of time, the player with more correct words wins.

un	pay	ful	less
tie	ing	pre	care
dis	wind	y	color
re	sun	over	er

©The Education Center, Inc. • Games Galore • Language Arts • TEC2516

Player:

Score:

Points																							
Words																							

"Purr-fect" Prefixes

Skill: using prefixes to make words

Number of players: 2

Materials:
- copy of page 58
- die
- 2 game pieces
- pencil
- lined paper for each student
- set of 15 prepared index cards
- marker
- dictionary

Teacher preparation:
1. Ahead of time, collect 15 3" x 5" lined index cards.
2. Divide the cards into five groups of three cards each.
3. Use a marker to program the blank sides of each group of cards with one of the following prefixes: *col-, con-, com-, co-,* and *cor-*.

Object of the game:

to be the first player to make ten words

Playing the game:
1. Shuffle the index cards and stack them facedown on the space labeled "Pick Up" on the gameboard.
2. Players place their game pieces on the START space of the gameboard.
3. To play, Player 1 rolls the die and then moves her game piece that number of spaces in either direction. Once on a space, Player 1 draws a card. Player 1 tries to make a word by matching her prefix card with the word ending shown on her space. Player 2 uses a dictionary to check Player 1's word. If it's correct, Player 1 writes the word on her paper. Then she places the prefix card facedown in a discard pile on the space labeled "Discard" on the gameboard. If her word is incorrect, she discards the card. Her turn is over.
4. Player 2 takes a turn in the same manner.
5. Play continues until one player has written ten words on her paper. That player is declared the winner.

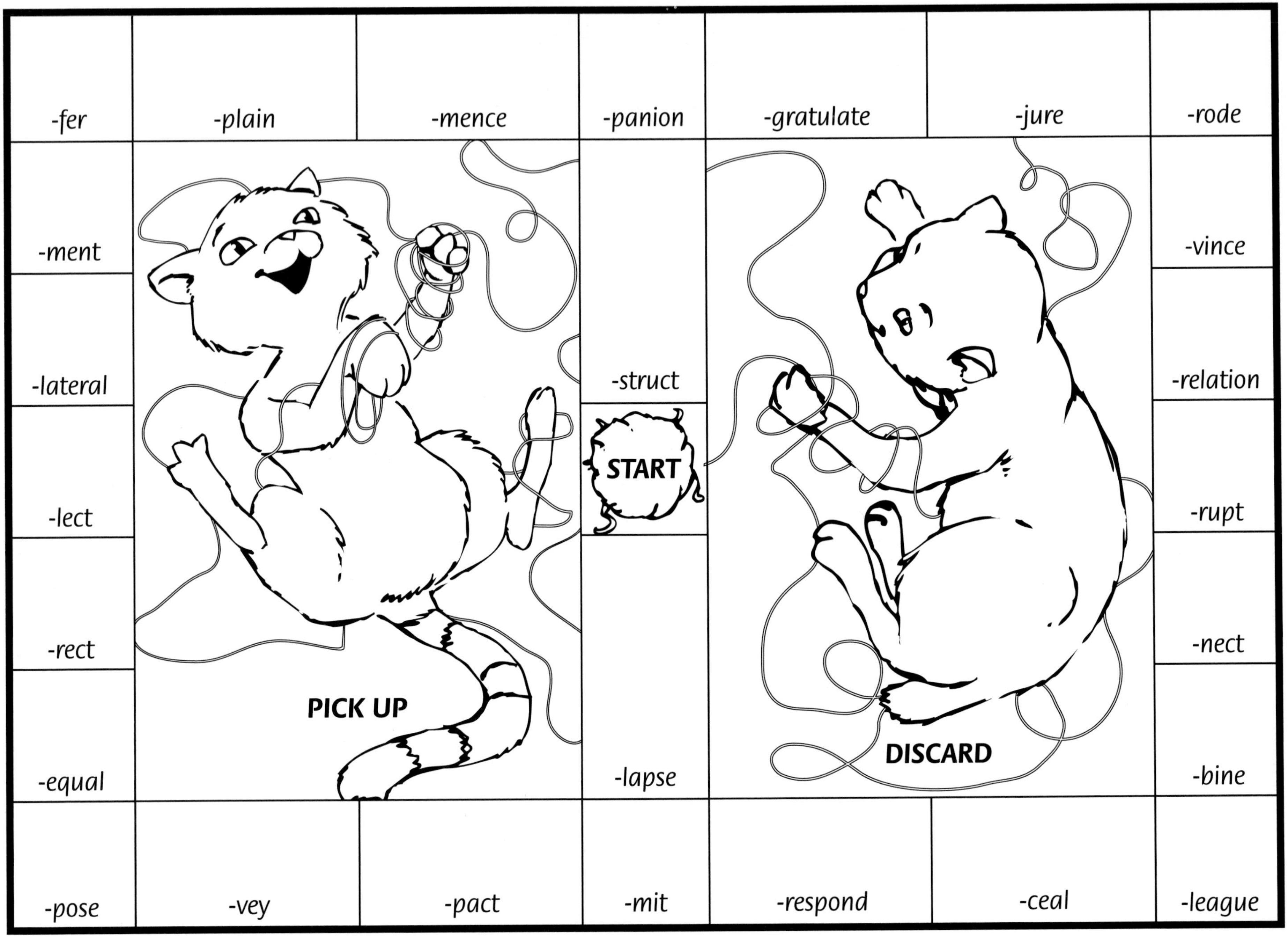

-rode

-vince

-relation

-rupt

-nect

-bine

-league

-jure

-ceal

DISCARD

-gratulate

-respond

-panion

-struct

START

-lapse

-mit

-mence

-pact

PICK UP

-plain

-vey

-fer

-ment

-lateral

-lect

-rect

-equal

-pose

Super Suffixes

Skill: forming words using suffixes

Number of players: 2

Materials:
- copy of page 60
- scissors
- die
- 6 self-adhesive dots
- marker
- dictionary
- small paper clip
- pencil for each player

Object of the game:

to correctly form more words by combining suffixes and base words

Playing the game:

1. Make a suffix cube by affixing a self-adhesive dot on each side of the die. Then use a marker to label each dot with one of the following suffixes: *-en, -ish, -ism, -ist, -ment,* or *-ness.*
2. To make a spinner, cut out the spinner pattern along the solid black line. Place a small paper clip in the middle of the spinner. Then stand a pencil in the paper clip with one hand and spin the clip with the other hand.
3. To play, Player 1 rolls the die and then spins the spinner. Player 1 reads the base word on the spinner and tries to add the suffix to it to create a new word. Player 2 uses the dictionary to check Player 1's word. If successful, Player 1 writes the word on the score sheet, along with her initials and the number of points indicated on the spinner. Then Player 1 takes another turn.
4. If Player 1 cannot create another word, then Player 2 takes a turn in the same manner.
5. Play continues until all of the lines on the score sheet are filled. Tally the number of points for each player. The player with more points is declared the winner.

©The Education Center, Inc.

Variation:

After adding a suffix to a base word, challenge students to identify the new word's part of speech.

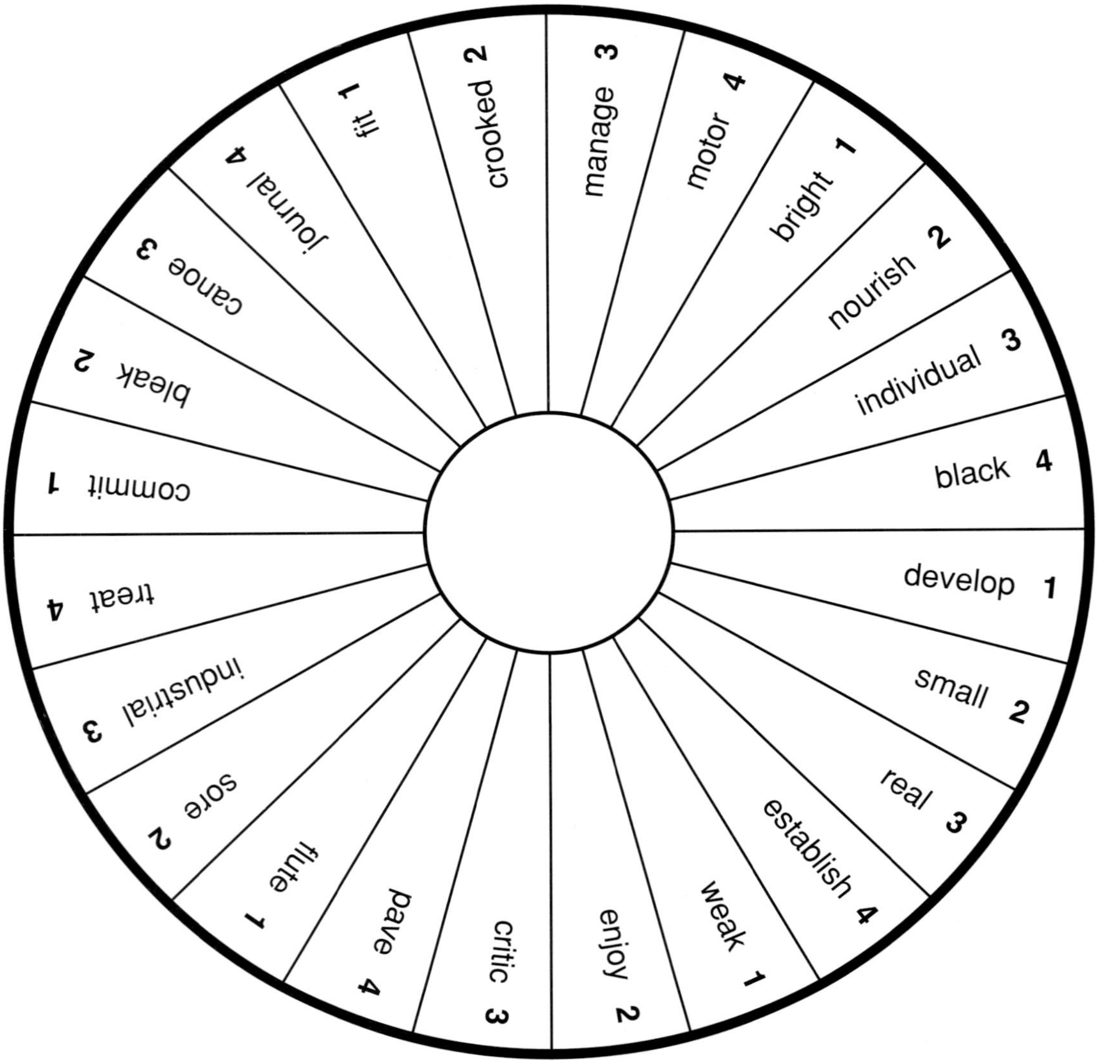

crooked 2
manage 3
motor 4
bright 1
nourish 2
individual 3
black 4
develop 1
small 2
real 3
establish 4
weak 1
enjoy 2
critic 3
pave 4
flute 1
sore 2
industrial 3
treat 4
commit 1
bleak 2
canoe 3
journal 4
fit 1

Created Word	Initial	Points

Jellyfish Jubilee

Skill: forming compound words

Number of players: 2

Materials:
- copy of page 62
- 2 pencils
- 2 sheets of paper
- dictionary
- watch

Object of the game:
to correctly identify and form more compound words

Playing the game:
1. Player 1 begins by circling a jellyfish.
2. Player 2 records as many compound words as possible using the circled word and the other words on the page. As Player 2 writes a word, he says it aloud. When Player 2 is finished making words, he calls out, "Jellyfish."
3. If Player 1 notices that Player 2 has missed a compound word, Player 1 "stings" Player 2 by writing any additional word combinations on his paper. If Player 1 agrees that no other words can be made, then Player 2 circles a word and Player 1 repeats Step 2. (Players may use a dictionary to check any questionable compound words.)
4. Play continues in this manner for 20 minutes or until all of the words have been circled. Players compare lists to be sure there aren't any duplicated words. No one earns points for duplicated words. Then each player counts the number of compound words on his list. The player who has created more compound words is declared the winner.

©The Education Center, Inc.

Variation:

To increase the number of players, make enough copies for each participant to have one. Have a player call out one of the jellyfish words and act as the timekeeper. The other students use that word to write as many compound words as possible in 30 seconds. When time is up, a different player calls out a word and acts as the timekeeper. When all of the words are circled, players check and total their words.

Jellyfish Jubilee

A Picture Is Worth...

Skill: forming compound words

Number of players: 2

Materials:
- copy of score sheets on page 64
- 2 sets of prepared picture clues
- timer or stopwatch
- dictionary for each player
- pencil for each player
- scissors

Teacher preparation:
1. Cut out and mount each picture clue on a small square of construction paper. Prepare two sets of cards.
2. Display the clues in a designated playing area.

Object of the game:
to correctly write as many compound words as possible in five minutes

Playing the game:
1. Cut apart the score sheets on page 64. Each player writes her name on a sheet.
2. Set the timer for five minutes.
3. Both players form compound words by combining a clue containing a word or picture with another clue containing a word or picture. Each player writes her compound words on her score sheet.
4. Play continues until time is up.
5. Players swap papers. Each player uses a dictionary to check the compound words.
6. One point is awarded for each correctly written compound word. Each player records her opponent's score on the score sheet. The player with the higher score is declared the winner.

©The Education Center, Inc.

Score Sheet

Player 1 _____

Score _____

Score Sheet

Player 2 _____

Score _____

Picture Clues

		light
	rise	half
	high	
	town	off
out		time

All Aboard!

Skill: defining commonly misused words

Number of players: 3

Materials:
- copy of page 66
- die
- 2 game pieces
- copy of the answer key on page 95

Object of the game:
to reach the finish space by correctly defining as many commonly misused words as possible

Playing the game:

1. Each player rolls the die. The player with the lowest roll will act as the "conductor." The other players will play the game.
2. Players place their game pieces on START.
3. Player 1 rolls the die, then moves that many spaces. Once there, Player 1 defines the word on the space. The conductor skims the answer key to determine if Player 1 has correctly defined the word. If so, the conductor allows Player 1 to roll again. If Player 1 incorrectly defines the next word, he moves back to his previous position on the gameboard. Then Player 2 takes a turn.
4. Play continues in this manner until one player reaches the finish space. The player who doesn't reach the finish space becomes the next conductor. The other students play the game as described above.
5. At the end of 30 minutes, the player who has reached the finish space the most times is declared the winner.

©The Education Center, Inc.

Variation:

Play as described above, except each student must correctly use the word on each space in a sentence.

All Aboard!

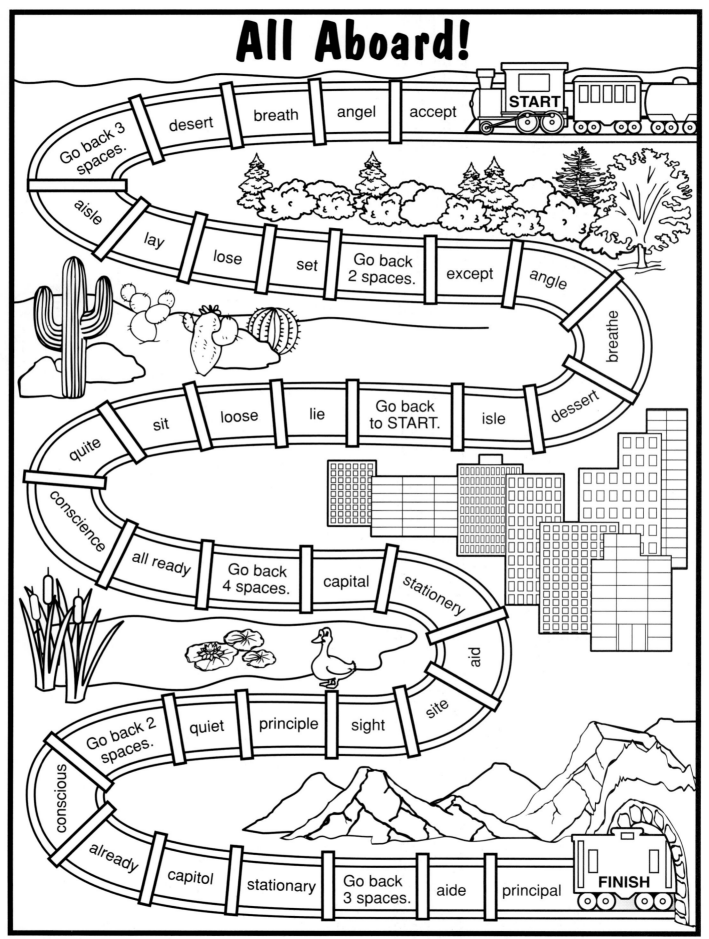

START

desert • breath • angel • accept

Go back 3 spaces. • aisle • lay • lose • set • Go back 2 spaces. • except • angle • breathe • dessert • isle • Go back to START. • lie • loose • sit • quite

conscience • all ready • Go back 4 spaces. • capital • stationery • aid • site • sight • principle • quiet • Go back 2 spaces.

conscious • already • capitol • stationary • Go back 3 spaces. • aide • principal • FINISH

One + One = One

Skill: identifying portmanteau words

Number of players: 4

Materials:
- 2 copies of page 68
- stopwatch or watch with a second hand
- 2 copies of the answer key on page 95
- 2 envelopes
- pencil for each player

Teacher preparation:
1. Place each answer key inside an envelope and seal it.
2. Give an envelope to each pair.

Object of the game:

to correctly identify as many portmanteau words as possible and the two words that make up each portmanteau in the lesser amount of time

Playing the game:
1. Set the stopwatch for three minutes.
2. To play, one member of each pair reads aloud a definition from page 68.
3. The other member locates the space containing the matching portmanteau word and the space containing the two words that make up the portmanteau word. Then he writes the letter of the definition in the triangle at the top, right-hand corner of each box.
4. Play continues in this manner until time is up. Then each pair opens its answer key envelope and checks its answers.
5. The pair with more correct answers is declared the winner.

Variation:

For a whole-group activity, divide students into two teams. Make a transparency of page 68; then assign each team a differently colored transparency marker. Play as directed except in turn, with a volunteer from each team. As teams locate the correct words, color the boxes with that team's transparency marker. When all of the words have been identified, the team with more colored boxes is declared the winner.

twist + whirl	splash + spatter	blotch	clash
fare + ye + well	brunch	gleam + shimmer	slosh
chortle	blot + botch	good-bye	taximeter + cabriolet
farewell	moped	motel	flash + gush
breakfast + lunch	twirl	clap + crash	flutter + hurry
clump	parachute + troops	telethon	flare
slop + slush	smash	motor + pedal	taxicab
flurry	chuckle + snort	splatter	television + marathon
God + be (with) + ye	squiggle	chunk + lump	flush
glimmer	flame + glare	smack + mash	by + cause
squirm + wriggle	because	paratroops	motor + hotel

A. for the reason that
B. a group of things close together
C. a place for lodging with a parking area easily reached from each room
D. to give a faint and unsteady light
E. a car used to carry passengers for a fare
F. a bicycle with a small motor
G. to scatter or fall as in drops
H. good wishes said when leaving
I. to chuckle with a sound like a snort
J. the slap or splash of liquid
K. to empty out with a sudden flow of water
L. to turn around rapidly
M. a loud, harsh noise
N. to blaze with a bright flame
O. to break into many pieces with noise or force
P. any large spot or stain
Q. a short curved or wavy line
R. to move in a confused manner
S. a television program lasting many hours that usually attempts to raise money for a charity
T. a word said when leaving someone
U. troops trained to parachute from an airplane
V. breakfast and lunch eaten as one meal late in the morning

Players _____

Score _____

Multiple Meanings

Skill: matching homographs

Number of players: 2

Materials:

- copy of page 70
- timer or watch with a second hand
- sealed envelope holding a copy of the answer key on page 95
- pencil for each player
- scissors

Object of the game:

to match more homographs in less time

Teacher preparation:

Seal a copy of the answer key inside an envelope for each pair.

Playing the game:

1. Cut apart the score sheets on page 70 and give one to each player.
2. After each player has written her name on the score sheet, set the timer for four minutes.
3. To play, players read each definition on their papers, locate the matching word in the box at the top of the score sheet, and then write the word number in the space beside the definition. Players continue playing in this manner until each word has been matched to two definitions.
4. When time is up, one player opens the envelope and reads the answers aloud. The player with more correct matches is declared the winner.

Variation:

Have players program several index cards, each with a homograph from page 70 or its definitions. Direct the players to spread out the cards facedown on the playing surface. In turn, have each player turn over three cards, trying to match the homograph with both definitions. Play continues until all of the cards have been matched. The player with more cards is declared the winner.

Player _____

1. trunk   5. fan   9. bridge
2. quarter 6. rest   10. fence
3. deal   7. tire   11. pen
4. box   8. tick   12. like

_____ device to stir the air
_____ agreement
_____ cardboard container
_____ light, recurring click
_____ to fight with swords
_____ similar to
_____ what is left
_____ main stem of a tree
_____ 25 cents
_____ to become weary
_____ writing instrument
_____ arachnid that sucks blood
_____ to fight with fists
_____ to be pleased with
_____ sleep
_____ type of card game
_____ barrier
_____ hoop of rubber around rim of wheel
_____ distribute cards
_____ elephant's long snout
_____ one-fourth of something
_____ enclosure for animals
_____ admirer
_____ structure over a river

Player _____

1. trunk   5. fan   9. bridge
2. quarter 6. rest   10. fence
3. deal   7. tire   11. pen
4. box   8. tick   12. like

_____ device to stir the air
_____ agreement
_____ cardboard container
_____ light, recurring click
_____ to fight with swords
_____ similar to
_____ what is left
_____ main stem of a tree
_____ 25 cents
_____ to become weary
_____ writing instrument
_____ arachnid that sucks blood
_____ to fight with fists
_____ to be pleased with
_____ sleep
_____ type of card game
_____ barrier
_____ hoop of rubber around rim of wheel
_____ distribute cards
_____ elephant's long snout
_____ one-fourth of something
_____ enclosure for animals
_____ admirer
_____ structure over a river

Stake a Claim

Skill: identifying synonyms and antonyms

Number of players: 2

Materials:
- copy of page 72
- set of prepared index cards
- dictionary
- pencil for each player

Object of the game:

to correctly identify more synonyms and antonyms

Teacher preparation:

1. Gather 30 index cards. Cut each card in half vertically.
2. Program one side of each index card with one of the synonyms or antonyms shown.

harmful	rotten	good		bare	blank	full
shiny	brilliant	dull		hot	burning	cold
debate	fight	agree		leave	exit	arrive
cautious	wary	careless		locate	discover	lose
mend	heal	break		tall	lofty	low
attractive	pretty	ugly		under	beneath	above
several	lots	sprinkling		call	yell	whisper
small	tiny	big		start	initiate	finish
fast	quick	slow		delayed	tardy	early
allowance	piece	whole		famished	ravenous	starving

Playing the game:

1. Shuffle the index cards. Deal 30 cards to each player. Each player places the cards facedown in a stack on the playing surface.
2. To play, Player 1 turns over one of her index cards. She looks at the gameboard and finds the best antonym or synonym for her word. Player 1 writes the word in one section of the correct space on the gameboard and signs her initials below the word. If Player 2 does not agree that the word has been written in the correct spot, then he looks the word up in the dictionary. If the word is incorrect, Player 1 must erase her word and place the index card on the bottom of her pile.
3. Player 2 takes a turn in the same manner.
4. When the last word in a section has been written, the player who has filled in more spaces writes her initials in the small center box.
5. Play continues until all of the boxes have been filled. The player with more initials on the board is declared the winner.

Stake a Claim!

□	□	□	□
hungry	fix	bad	bright
□	□	□	□
argue	careful	beautiful	many
□	□	□	□
little	rapid	portion	empty
□	□	□	□
boiling	depart	find	high
□	□	□	□
below	shout	begin	late

Leapin' Lily Pads

Skill: writing synonyms and antonyms

Number of players: 4

Materials:
- copy of page 74
- scissors
- glue
- pencil for each player

Object of the game:

to correctly write the most synonyms and antonyms

Playing the game:
1. Assemble the die pattern as directed on page 74.
2. To play, Player 1 rolls the die and then writes either a synonym or an antonym for *good* in the space provided. If successful, Player 1 records the number of points on the die next to the word in her column. If Player 1 can't write a synonym or antonym, then she places an X in the space.
3. Player 2 rolls the die. She tries to write either a synonym or antonym for Player 1's word. If Player 1 was unable to write a word, then Player 2 writes a synonym or antonym for the previous word. If successful, Player 2 records the number of points on the die in the space next to her word. If unsuccessful, she marks an X in her space.
4. Players cannot repeat words already written.
5. Play continues in this manner until all of the spaces on the page have been filled. Players tally their points. The player with the most points is declared the winner.

Directions:

1. Carefully cut out the die pattern along the outside edges.
2. Place the pattern printed side up on your desk. Fold along the uncut solid lines to form a cube. (The words should be on the outside of the die.)
3. Glue the tabs to the inside of the die.

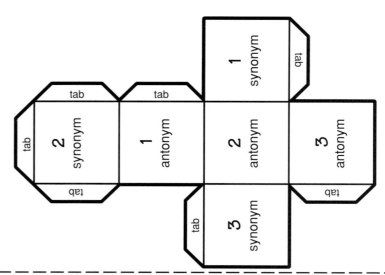

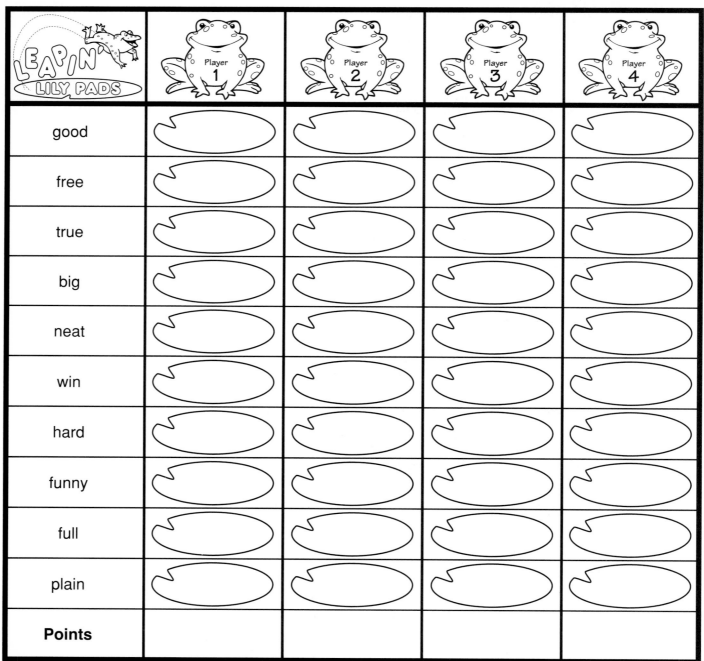

LEAPIN' LILY PADS	Player 1	Player 2	Player 3	Player 4
good				
free				
true				
big				
neat				
win				
hard				
funny				
full				
plain				
Points				

Homophone Home Run

Skill: using homophones

Number of players: 2

Materials:
- copy of page 76
- die
- 2 game pieces
- dictionary
- pencil for each player
- lined paper for each player

Object of the game:

to correctly use more homophones and earn more runs

HOMOPHONE HOME RUNS

Score	Score
III	ﬀﬀﬀ

Playing the game:

1. Place the game pieces on the home plate marker.
2. Player 1 rolls the die and then moves her game piece the indicated number of spaces. Once on the space, Player 1 writes a sentence for each homophone shown.
3. Player 2 checks Player 1's sentences using the dictionary for help. If Player 1 is correct, she moves to the next base. If Player 1 is incorrect, she moves back to the previous base.
4. In turn, each player rolls the die, writes sentences, and moves around the gameboard. Each time a player passes home plate, she makes a tally mark on the scoreboard.
5. Players cannot repeat sentences that have already been written.
6. At the end of 30 minutes, the player with more "runs" on the scoreboard is declared the winner.

©The Education Center, Inc.

Variation:

Have students begin on home plate. One player moves along the right-hand side of the board. The other player moves along the left-hand side of the board. Players race to correctly define the words on their respective sides of the board. The player with more correct definitions is declared the winner.

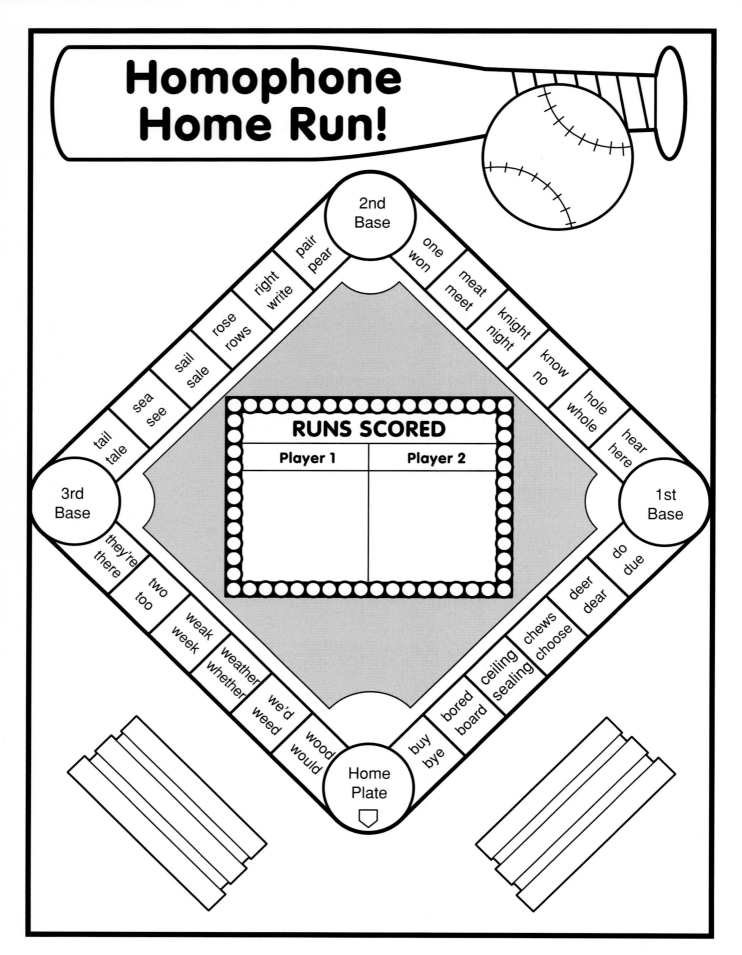

Homophone Home Run!

2nd Base

pair / pear
right / write
rose / rows
sail / sale
sea / see
tail / tale

one / won
meat / meet
knight / night
know / no
hole / whole
hear / here

RUNS SCORED
Player 1	Player 2

3rd Base

they're / there
two / too
weak / week
weather / whether
we'd / weed
wood / would

1st Base

do / due
deer / dear
chews / choose
ceiling / sealing
bored / board
buy / bye

Home Plate

Pack a Picnic

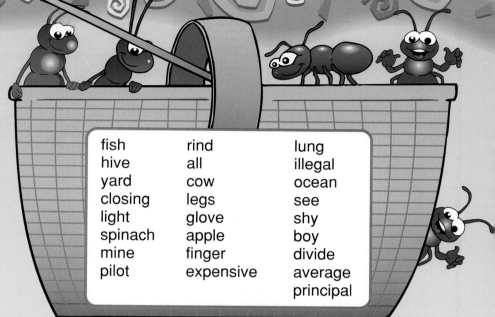

Skill: identifying analogies

Number of players: 2–4

fish   rind   lung
hive   all   illegal
yard   cow   ocean
closing   legs   see
light   glove   shy
spinach   apple   boy
mine   finger   divide
pilot   expensive   average
                        principal

Materials:
- copy of page 78
- 2 dice
- 2 game pieces
- prepared index cards

Teacher preparation:
1. Gather thirteen 3" x 5" index cards. Cut each card in half vertically.
2. Program one side of each index card with one of the words shown. (There will be one unused card half.)

Object of the game:
to collect the most word cards by completing the most analogies

Playing the game:
1. Stack the word cards in a pile facedown on the gameboard.
2. Each player places his game piece on the start space.
3. Player 1 rolls the dice and moves the indicated number of spaces horizontally and/or vertically (not diagonally) along the gameboard.
4. If Player 1 lands on a food space, no action is taken and it becomes Player 2's turn. If Player 1 lands on an analogy space, he reads the analogy aloud and takes the number of cards he rolled on the dice. Player 1 reads each card. If he holds a card that completes the analogy, he keeps the card. Remaining cards are returned to the bottom of the pile. Once an analogy has been completed, mark that space with an X. The square is now out of play.
5. Players take turns in the same manner.
6. Play continues for 30 minutes. The player with the most cards is declared the winner.

Variation:

To make the game more challenging, direct students to think of words that will complete each analogy rather than using the game cards.

Add is to subtract as multiply is to _____ .

Legal is to _____ as proper is to improper.

Bread is to crust as lemon is to _____ .

Fish is to gill as kitten is to _____ .

Ship is to captain as plane is to _____ .

Teacher is to classroom as _____ is to school.

Yellow is to lemon as red is to _____ .

Ear is to hear as eye is to _____ .

Puppy is to dog as calf is to _____ .

Centimeter is to meter as inch is to _____ .

Peach is to fruit as _____ is to vegetable.

Minimal is to maximum as cheap is to _____ .

Sister is to girl as brother is to _____ .

Oil is to well as gold is to _____ .

Bird is to nest as bee is to _____ .

Foot is to shoe as hand is to _____ .

Granite is to rock as guppy is to _____ .

Few is to many as some is to _____ .

Brave is to courageous as timid is to _____ .

Common is to extra-ordinary as usual is to _____ .

Begin is to end as opening is to _____ .

Toe is to foot as _____ to hand.

START

Sing is to voice as dance is to _____ .

Chocolate is to vanilla as dark is to _____ .

Whale is to _____ as monkey is to jungle.

CARDS

Sounds Like a Simile

Skill: writing similes

Number of players: 2

Materials:

- copy of page 80
- 2 dice
- 6 self-adhesive dots
- marker
- 2 game pieces
- 2 pencils

Object of the game:

to write more sentences using similes

The dog was as light as a feather when she picked him up.

Playing the game:

1. Make a noun die by labeling two self-adhesive dots with the word *person,* two with the word *place,* and two with the word *thing.* Then affix one dot to each side of the die.
2. Position the gameboard so that each player can easily write sentences in his spaces. Player 1 should note that his game spaces are gray, while Player 2 should note that his game spaces are white. If a player lands on a space that is not his own, he loses a turn.
3. To play, each player places his game piece on one of his spaces on the gameboard.
4. Player 1 rolls the dice and moves his game piece the number of spaces shown on the number die. Then he reads aloud the words in the space and the category on the noun die. He tries to create a sentence using the noun category to complete the simile. (For example, if he lands on the space *as hungry as* and rolls *thing,* he could say "Leo was as hungry as a lion.") If Player 2 agrees that the sentence makes sense, Player 1 records it on one of the lines on his side of the gameboard.
5. Player 2 takes a turn in the same manner.
6. The player who fills his side of the gameboard with sentences first is declared the winner.

Variation:

Allow students to write sentences for any spaces on the gameboard. Have the players turn the gameboard to read the words in the space if necessary.

Player 1

- as light as
- as soft as
- as lovely as
- walks like
- as quick as
- as happy as
- laughs like
- as sweet as
- as hard as
- as strong as
- as dry as
- works like
- as sly as
- as pretty as
- as cute as

Player 2

- moves like
- as comfortable as
- stood out like
- as smooth as
- as rough as
- as flat as
- as quiet as
- as hungry as
- slept like
- as rich as
- sparkled like
- as green as
- eats like
- as skinny as
- as deep as

All About Alliteration

Skill: writing sentences using alliteration

Number of players: 2

Materials:
- copy of page 82
- glue
- small paper clip
- pencil for each player
- lined paper for each player

Object of the game:

to earn more points for writing sentences using alliteration

Playing the game:

1. Make a number cube by following the directions on page 82.
2. To make a spinner, cut out the spinner pattern on page 82 along the heavy solid line. Place a small paper clip in the middle of the spinner. Then stand a pencil in the paper clip with one hand and spin the clip with the other hand.
3. To play, Player 1 rolls the number cube and spins the spinner. Then she writes an alliterative sentence using the letter shown on the spinner. Player 1 tries to write as many words that begin with that letter as she rolled on the die. (For example, if Player 1 rolled a 4 on the die and spun an *m* on the spinner, she would try to write a sentence with four words that begin with the consonant *m*.) To make sense, sentences may need a few words that do not begin with the consonant spun.
4. After Player 1 writes her sentence, she shows it to Player 2. Player 2 awards Player 1 a point for every word that has the beginning consonant spun. Points are recorded at the end of each sentence.
5. Player 2 takes a turn in the same manner.
6. At the end of 25 minutes, the player with more points is declared the winner.

Directions for making a cube:
1. Cut out the cube pattern along the heavy solid line.
2. Fold the pattern along each dotted line to form a cube.
3. Glue each tab inside the cube.

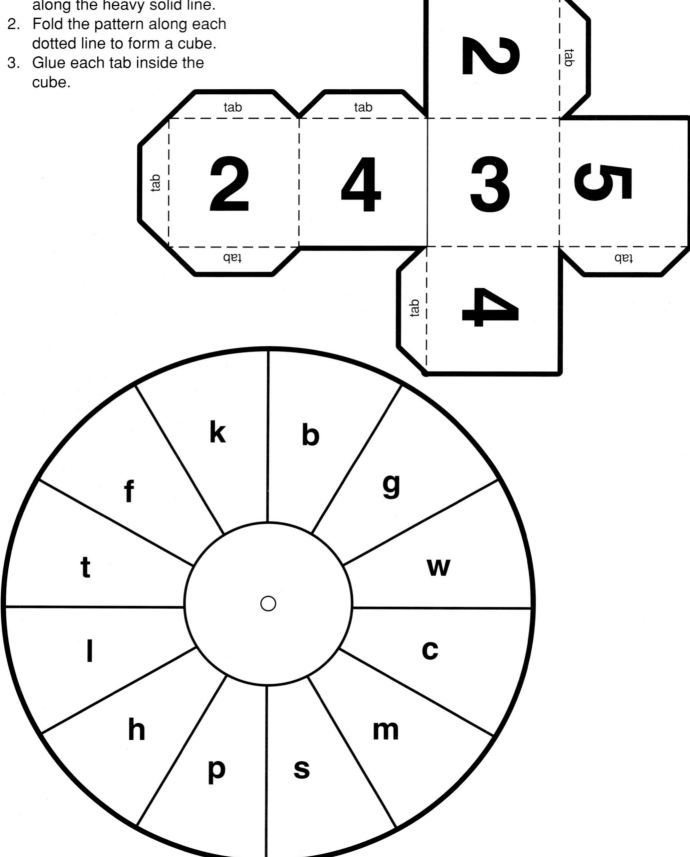

©The Education Center, Inc. • *Games Galore* • *Language Arts* • TEC2516

The Education Center®

TEC2516

From Your Friends at THE MAILBOX®

Grades 4-6

Games Galore

LANGUAGE ARTS

Skill-Based **Games** That Make Learning **Fun**

- Reinforces language arts skills
- Helps students feel successful
- Designed for partners, small groups, or the whole class

Triple-Scoop Grammar Gameboard

All Aboard!

Enhance Their Language Arts and Writing Skills

Power Practice Language Arts
100 Engaging Reproducible Activities to Build Basic Skills

Our fun formats will inspire students to learn basic skills with innovative, standards-based activities. Child-centered activities feature engaging graphics and high-interest topics for learning success. 112 pages.

TEC 2668.   Grades 4–6

Grammar Plus!
Supports IRA/NCTE Standards

Hook your students on using good grammar with creative lessons that support curriculum standards. Grades 4–6. 48 pages.

TEC 2313.   Capitalization & Punctuation
TEC 2314.   Sentence Structure & Usage
TEC 2315.   Parts of Speech

730 Journal Prompts

A full year of exciting journal topics that will give your students an enthusiasm for writing. 112 pages.

TEC 3170.   Grades 1–3
TEC 3171.   Grades 4–6

Writing Works!™
Easy-to-Implement, Curriculum-Based Writing Lessons!

Develop and enhance your students' writing competence with this valuable resource of step-by-step lessons. Grades 4–6. 48 pages.

TEC 2307.   Narrative
TEC 2308.   Clarification
TEC 2309.   Descriptive
TEC 2310.   Persuasive
TEC 2311.   Explanatory
TEC 2312.   Expressive

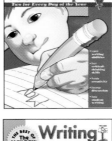

The Best of *The Mailbox* Writing

Everything you need to make writing more fun, including creative-writing activities, journal topics, bulletin boards, and unique "Our Readers Write" tips from *The Mailbox*. 112 pages.

TEC 1485.   Grades 4–6

The Best of *The Mailbox* Language Arts

Organized by skill so that you can find the exact activity you need, this is an easy-to-use resource for teaching basic language arts skills. 160 pages.

TEC 1459.   Grades 1–3
TEC 1460.   Grades 4–6

Mind Builders—Language Arts and Vocabulary & Spelling
Daily Problems and Puzzles to Strengthen Critical-Thinking Skills

Reinforce your language arts and vocabulary-building curriculum in a challenging and fun way while strengthening critical-thinking skills. Look for Mind Builders in other curriculum areas as well! 48 pages.

TEC 1603.   Language Arts (Grade 1)
TEC 1604.   Language Arts (Grade 2)
TEC 1605.   Language Arts (Grade 3)
TEC 1607.   Language Arts (Grades 4–6)
TEC 1610.   Vocabulary & Spelling (Grades 4–6)

Lifesaver Lessons®
Language Arts
Ready-to-Go Lesson Plans

Creative, curriculum-based step-by-step lessons. Great for teachers who need a last-minute lesson, substitutes, and first-time teachers alike. 96 pages.

TEC 492.   Grade 1   TEC 495.   Grade 4
TEC 493.   Grade 2   TEC 496.   Grade 5
TEC 494.   Grade 3

Ask for books from *The Mailbox* at your local school supply store.

Incredible Idioms

Skill: matching idioms with their meanings

Number of players: 2

Materials:
- copy of page 84
- 40 3" x 5" index cards
- scissors
- glue

Object of the game:

to match more idioms with their meanings

Wow! Sue was really burned up about the game.

Playing the game:
1. Cut apart the boxes on page 84 along the solid black lines. Then glue each card to one side of an index card.
2. Shuffle the cards and deal seven cards to each player. Stack the remaining cards in a pile facedown on the playing surface.
3. To play, Player 1 matches within her hand any idiom sentence card to its meaning card. Player 1 lays down all matches and then draws another card. If the card drawn creates a match, she lays the pair down. Then Player 1 discards an unmatched card from her hand, laying it faceup in the discard pile.
4. Player 2 takes a turn in the same manner, except she can choose to pick up the entire discard pile instead of drawing a card.
5. Play continues until one person uses all of her cards. The player with more matched cards is declared the winner.

©The Education Center, Inc.

Variation:

Remove the meaning cards from the deck. Stack the remaining cards faceup on the playing surface. Provide players with a stopwatch or a watch with a second hand. Players race to correctly say the meaning of each idiom card.

The man told me to hold my tongue.	Please put your John Hancock on the dotted line.	Get it clean. Use a little elbow grease.	That guy really gets on my nerves.
Before giving a speech, I always get cold feet.	When he didn't get picked, Sam looked down in the dumps.	Becky thought the test was a piece of cake.	My grandfather is 90 years old, but he's fit as a fiddle.
Danny, can you give me a hand?	Wow! Sue was really burned up.	Getting second place is nothing to sneeze at.	Kyle will show you the ropes.
To be successful, we need to stick together.	David got up on the wrong side of the bed this morning.	I'd give my right arm for a piece of chocolate cake.	The test score showed that Jed never cracked a book.
I thought you had lost your marbles when you said you saw a purple hippopotamus.	Sarah let the cat out of the bag by telling Jade about the party.	Tanya made it this far, but she wasn't out of the woods yet.	The trip seemed to take forever and a day.
Discouraged	Safe from danger	A long time	Gone crazy
Stay together	Awoke in a bad mood	Make a sacrifice	Studied
Signature	Be silent	Energy	Lose courage
Annoys me	Told a secret	Not difficult	In good health
Help me	Angry	Not to be taken lightly	Teach you

Abbreviation Station

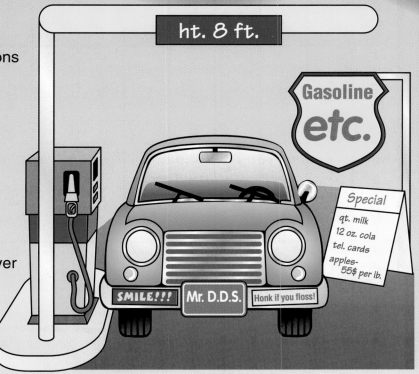

ht. 8 ft.

Gasoline
etc.

Special
qt. milk
12 oz. cola
tel. cards
apples-
55$ per lb.

SMILE!!! Mr. D.D.S. Honk if you floss!

Skill: identifying common abbreviations

Number of players: 2

Materials:
- copy of page 86
- die
- copy of the answer key on page 96
- white letter-sized envelope
- pencil of a different color for each player
- timer

Teacher preparation:
1. Place the answer key inside the envelope and seal it.
2. Give the envelope to the players before they begin the game.

Object of the game:
to earn more points for identifying common abbreviations

Playing the game:
1. Player 2 sets the timer for 15 seconds.
2. Player 1 rolls the die to determine the number of words she will match to their abbreviations. Then she colors the appropriate number of abbreviation boxes and marks off the corresponding words with her colored pencil.
3. Player 2 takes a turn in the same manner while Player 1 keeps time.
4. When all of the words and abbreviations have been matched, players open the envelope and check their matches. Next, each player's points are totaled, with one point being awarded for each correct match. The player with more points is declared the winner.

©The Education Center, Inc.

Variation:

Cut the words from the page. Then challenge players to write the word that matches each abbreviation on a sheet of paper. Score the game as directed above.

adj.	biog.	cm	D.D.S.
dept.	doz.	ea.	etc.
F	ft.	Fri.	g
gal	Gen.	govt.	hosp.
hr.	ht.	in.	inc.
intro	Jr.	kg	lat.
lb.	long.	mag.	math
M.D.	med.	min.	misc.
ml	Mr.	Mrs.	oz.
p.	pkg.	pop.	pt.
Pres.	qt.	R.N.	sci.
sec.	sq.	subj.	tel.
vol.	wk.	wt.	yd.
	yr.	vocab.	

General
centimeter
Doctor of Dental Surgery
vocabulary
pound
introduction
package
square
biography
miscellaneous
Fahrenheit
hospital
magazine
ounce
weight
Mister
milliliter
foot
gram
department
inch
week
medium
page
quart
telephone
incorporated

subject
kilogram
adjective
mathematics
Friday
President
Registered Nurse
gallon
year
each
hour
minute
Junior
height
yard
pint
government
Mistress
latitude
Doctor of Medicine
et cetera (and others)
population
science
second
longitude
dozen
volume

Make a Match

Skill: identifying hink pinks

Number of players: 2

Materials:
- copy of page 88
- 48 bingo chips or other small counters (divided into 2 different-colored groups of 24 counters each)
- die
- stopwatch or watch with a second hand
- lined paper for each player
- pencil for each player

Object of the game:

to identify more hink pinks

vehicle carrying quacking animals

DUCK TRUCK

Playing the game:
1. Player 1 rolls the die.
2. Player 2 sets the stopwatch for 15 seconds. Player 1 places one of her counters on a definition space on the gameboard. Then she locates the matching hink pink and places a counter on the hink pink space before time runs out.
3. If the hink pink and definition are matched in time, Player 1 records the number rolled as the number of points earned for her turn. If Player 1 cannot locate the hink pink within the time limit, the number rolled is recorded as a negative score to be deducted from any points earned in the next turn.
4. Player 2 takes a turn in the same manner while Player 1 acts as the time-keeper.
5. Play continues until all of the hink pinks are identified. The player with more points is declared the winner.

©The Education Center, Inc.

Make a Match

clever prank	rabbit with a sense of humor	a journey by boat	skinny arm or leg	cook who cannot hear	messy reproduction
untamed kid	group that eats together	without money	very thin horse	sound slumber	home for a rodent
mad employer	unhappy father	overweight feline	ill poultry	noisy mob	lengthy tune
nice gift	shining sun	entrance to a shop	large hog	seat for a rabbit	skinny hotel

big pig	mouse house	sick chick	sloppy copy	slick trick	slim limb
pleasant present	funny bunny	sad dad	ship trip	deep sleep	store door
thin inn	bony pony	long song	fat cat	deaf chef	bright light
loud crowd	no dough	cross boss	hare chair	lunch bunch	wild child

Gridlock

Skill: using words to make sentences

Number of players: 2

Materials:
- copy of page 90
- 2 dice
- stopwatch or watch with a second hand
- pencil for each player
- lined paper for each player

Object of the game:

to earn more points for writing sentences

Playing the game:

1. Player 1 rolls the dice. Player 1 locates the words on the grid that correspond to the numbers rolled. For example, if Player 1 rolls a 1 and a 6, he locates the first space in the sixth row (grapefruit) and the sixth space in the first row (brave).
2. Player 2 sets the stopwatch for ten seconds.
3. Player 1 writes a sentence on his paper using the words from both spaces. If his sentence is completed before time is up, Player 1 makes an X on both spaces on the grid. These words are now off-limits and unusable. The player makes a tally mark in his score box.
4. If a double is rolled, the player uses the word(s) on the grid at that position and chooses another word(s) on the grid to use in his sentence. If a player rolls the dice and the word(s) on at least one position has already been used, it becomes the next player's turn.
5. All players take turns in the same manner.
6. Play continues until the grid is locked (all the words have been used). The player with more points is declared the winner.

Variation:

Provide a pair of different-colored dice. Designate one die for rows and the other die for columns. Direct each player to roll the dice twice to determine two coordinates on the grid. Then have students play as directed above.

White-out the words on the grid. Have students write a vocabulary word in each box. Then have students play as directed above.

	1	2	3	4	5	6
6	grapefruit	whisper	best friend	kitchen	oink	igloo
5	lifeguard	Uncle Charlie	turkey	above	red roses	piano
4	mysterious	Ireland	garbage truck	penguin	giggling	purple
3	billboard	grandfather clock	plumber	downstairs	chocolate milk	kitten
2	birthday cake	empty suitcase	White House	correct	pilot	noisy
1	vacuum cleaner	diamond necklace	starving	waddle	necktie	brave

| **1** | **2** | **3** | **4** | **5** | **6** |

Player 1 _____   **Player 2** _____

Shelves of Surprises

Skill: differentiating fact from opinion

Number of players: 2

Materials:

- copy of page 92
- die
- 2 game pieces
- 2 index cards for each player
- pencil for each player
- white letter-sized envelope
- copy of the answer key on page 96

Teacher preparation:

1. Place the answer key inside the envelope and seal it.
2. Give the envelope to the players before they begin the game.

Object of the game:

to be the first to "check out" six fact-based and six opinion-based books

Playing the game:

1. Players label one index card "Fact" and the other card "Opinion." Then each player numbers each card from 1 to 6.
2. Players place their game pieces on the start space on the gameboard.
3. Player 1 rolls the die and moves his game piece that number of spaces. After reading the title of the book, Player 1 decides whether the book is most likely factual or based on the author's opinion. Then Player 1 "checks out" the book by writing the title on one of his index cards.
4. Player 2 takes a turn in the same manner. Players may not record the same titles. If a player lands on a book that has been checked out by another player, he loses his turn.
5. Play continues until a player checks out six fact-based books and six opinion-based books. The first player to do so is declared the winner.

Variation:

Add a point value to each book title. As students check out the books, have them note the number of points each book is worth on their index cards. At the end of the game, have the students tally up their points to determine the winner.

Talk to Your Kids About Drugs	Planting Perennials	All Fears Are Silly	Girls Don't Make Good Athletes	Telling Time	Believing You Are Wonderful	Cheetahs Run; Snakes Wait	Hurricanes and Tornadoes	I Love My Dog	Marathons Are Meaningless

Rocks and Minerals	Dads Don't Dance	Cooking Tex-Mex Style	Boys Can't Make Cookies	American Ecosystems	Tennis Is Tops	Math Is for Smarties	All About Aardvarks	Animals' Camouflage	Fourth Grade Hurts

1942: A Year in Pictures	Science Is the Coolest	Remodel Your Kitchen	101 Arts and Crafts	The Nicest Teachers Are Tall	Math for Beginners	Principals Make Great Pasta	Growing Herb Gardens	Good Grades Don't Make You Smart	Ferrets Don't Make Good Pets

Be Resourceful

Skill: determining appropriate resources

Number of players: 2–4

Materials:
- copy of page 94
- die
- game pieces
- set of 30 prepared resource cards

Teacher preparation:
1. Cut fifteen 3" x 5" index cards in half vertically.
2. Divide the cards into five groups of six cards each. Program the blank sides of the cards in each group with one of the following resources: *dictionary, encyclopedia, atlas, current newspaper,* and *almanac.*

Object of the game:
to be the first player to use all of her resource cards

Playing the game:
1. Shuffle the resource cards and deal four cards to each player. Stack the remaining cards on the resource pile space on the gameboard.
2. Players place their game pieces on the start space.
3. Player 1 rolls the die and moves the indicated number of spaces in any direction on the board. She reads the information on her space and determines the type of resource needed to locate that information. If she has the card in her hand, she places it on the discard pile space on the gameboard. If she doesn't hold the correct card, she draws a card from the resource pile.
4. Player 2 takes a turn in the same manner.
5. If there are no more cards in the resource pile, the discard pile is shuffled and placed facedown in the resource pile space on the gameboard.
6. The player who uses all of her resource cards first is declared the winner.

| Today's temperature | Definition of a word | Article about a local robbery | Mexico's major exports | Countries surrounding Nigeria | LOSE A TURN | Facts about the American Revolution |

| Capital city of a country | **Be Resourceful.** | | Number of syllables in a word | RESOURCE PILE | | Up-to-date stock prices |

List of United Nations members

LOSE A TURN

Current population information

TAKE A RESOURCE CARD

Birthplace of a 19th-century president

Pronunciation of a word

| Last night's baseball game scores | History of a country | START | | Favorite comic strip | History of a word |

| MOVE ONE SPACE IN ANY DIRECTION | DISCARD PILE | | Winners of last year's Academy Awards | **Reap Rewards.** | | Yesterday's sports scores |

Average temperature of a city

Tomorrow's weather forecast

Outcome of last year's elections

Rivers within a country's borders

Distance between two cities

ROLL AGAIN

| Listing of pets for sale | Facts about dinosaurs | Size of largest trout ever caught | GIVE A CARD TO ANOTHER PLAYER | Word's part of speech | Time of favorite TV show | Lifetime batting average of favorite baseball player |

Answer Keys

Page 28

1.	compound	6.	compound	11.	simple	16.	complex
2.	complex	7.	compound	12.	complex	17.	compound
3.	compound	8.	complex	13.	complex	18.	simple
4.	complex	9.	simple	14.	simple	19.	simple
5.	simple	10.	compound	15.	simple	20.	simple

Page 38

Answers may vary because of the inflection given by a player, but generally, answers are as follows:

The competition is at 10:00.	Help me do my stretches.
Shall we meet at 8:00?	Our team will perform first.
Let's go in a little early.	Is everyone here?
How nervous I am!	Look at how good that other team is!
Get on the bus at the corner.	Let's try to do our best.
Where shall we sit?	I will be next.
Take the back seat the best.	Wish me luck!
How bumpy this street is!	Did it look as good as I thought?
Go to check in first.	What a relief it is that it's over!
Is this where our team meets?	I'm sure you'll do just as well.
What a huge gym this is!	Hang in there!
Need to warm up.	What a super performance that was!
Think my bag is on the bench.	Don't you feel great?
How clumsy I feel!	Make sure you have your medal.
What if I fall during my event?	What a great day this is!

Page 40

Susan bought popcorn, soda, a hot dog, and chips at the game.
Wow! My aunt lives in Calgary, too.
Emma, when was the last time you saw Jeff?
The package contained a yo-yo, puzzle, cassette tape, and book.
Well, are you coming to the game?
Mr. Sherman is a doctor, and he owns his own Internet business.
It was a cold, rainy, windy night.
I think I saw him yesterday, Kate.
Mrs. Sherman is a nurse, and she has a degree in business.
Jerry, Kim, and Nancy need to take lessons this summer.
Ryan, Brendan, and Tara are expert swimmers.
"No, I think I will stay home."
"Will you leave tomorrow, Albert?"
My best subjects are reading, Spanish, science, and history.
I did well in math, science, health, and reading.
We returned to Oakland, California, on May 26, 2001.
My birthday is April 17, 1991.
Yes, and I will take Lena with me, Rose.
My pen pal, Kendra, lives in Calgary, Alberta.
He drove an old, rusty, secondhand car to the theater.
We left for Tampa, Florida, on March 16, 2002.
I was born on July 3, 1990.

Page 46

"We're just trying to keep our heads above water," piped the plumbers jointly.
"It's a dog-eat-dog world!" barked the veterinarian impatiently.
The firefighter screeched hotly, "You're just adding fuel to the fire!"
The actor heartily recited, "All the world's a stage."
"If the shoe's too big," giggled the clown ridiculously, "wear it!"
"Too many cooks spoil the broth," admitted the chef tastelessly.
"I'll have ham and cheese on rye," ordered the judge decidedly, "and hold the mustard."
"If at first you don't succeed," instructed the teacher learnedly, "try, try again."
"Don't cry," babbled the baby wisely, "over spilled milk."
"Romeo, Romeo," quoted Shakespeare playfully, "wherefore art thou?"
The mime thought, "Silence is golden?"
"Honestly, Princess," croaked the frog jumpily, "there's no reason to kiss me!"
"Let's not split hairs over it!" clipped the barber sharply.
Shockingly, the electrician snapped, "We're getting down to the wire!"
"Catch you later," panted the runner breathlessly.
"Put your money," guessed the contestant unsurely, "where your mouth is?"

Page 50

B.	1.	a lot
C.	2.	their
	3.	stories
D.	1.	author
E.	2.	chosen
	5.	getting
F.	1.	Wednesday
	5.	coming
G.	2.	governor
	3.	finally
	6.	forty
H.	1.	boxes
	6.	children
I.	2.	truly
	3.	Saturday
	5.	fifteen
J.	2.	ninety
	6.	except
K.	2.	wolves
	3.	believe
	6.	forest
L.	1.	separate
	3.	February
	6.	describe
M.	3.	because
	4.	vegetable
	6.	always
N.	2.	dropping
	4.	chief
O.	1.	argument
P.	1.	knowledge
	3.	chocolate
	4.	calendar
	6.	hoping
Q.	2.	guard
	4.	college
	6.	doesn't
R.	2.	Tuesday
	3.	attendance
	5.	committee
	6.	hundred
S.	1.	beginning
	3.	business
	4.	familiar
T.	2.	government
	4.	special
U.	2.	leaves
	4.	awful
V.	1.	usually
	4.	field
W.	5.	biscuit

Page 66

accept—to agree or take what is offered
aid—the act of helping
aide—a person who acts as an assistant
aisle—a passage separating rows of seats
all ready—completely ready
already—even now or by this time
angel—heavenly body
angle—space between two lines that meet in a point
breathe—to inhale and exhale
breath—respiration
capital—chief in importance or influence
capitol—a building where a state legislative body meets
conscience—sense of right and wrong
conscious—aware
desert—arid land
dessert—course served at the end of a meal
except—leaving out or excluding
isle—an island
lay—to set something down or place something
lie—to recline
loose—not tight
lose—to not win; to misplace
principal—person with controlling authority
principle—a rule
quiet—not noisy
quite—very
set—to place in or on
sight—the process, power, or function of seeing
sit—to rest on one's haunches
site—the area or planned location of a structure
stationary—fixed in a position
stationery—writing materials

Page 68

A. by + cause, because
B. chunk + lump, clump
C. motor + hotel, motel
D. gleam + shimmer, glimmer
E. taximeter + cabriolet, taxicab
F. motor + pedal, moped
G. splash + spatter, splatter
H. fare + ye + well, farewell
I. chuckle + snort, chortle
J. slop + slush, slosh
K. flash + gush, flush
L. twist + whirl, twirl
M. clap + crash, clash
N. flame + glare, flare
O. smack + mash, smash
P. blot + botch, blotch
Q. squirm + wriggle, squiggle
R. flutter + hurry, flurry
S. television + marathon, telethon
T. God + be (with) + ye, good-bye
U. parachute + troops, paratroops
V. breakfast + lunch, brunch

Page 70

5	device to stir the air		4	to fight with fists
3	agreement		12	to be pleased with
4	cardboard container		6	sleep
8	light, recurring click		9	type of card game
10	to fight with swords		10	barrier
12	similar to		7	hoop of rubber around rim of wheel
6	what is left		3	distribute cards
1	main stem of a tree		1	elephant's long snout
2	25 cents		2	one-fourth of something
7	to become weary		11	enclosure for animals
11	writing instrument		5	admirer
8	arachnid that sucks blood		9	structure over a river

Project Manager: Cindy Mondello
Staff Editors: Diane F. McGraw, Jennifer Munnerlyn
Contributing Writers: Julia Alarie, Michelle Bauml, Diane Coffman, Rusty Fischer, Ann Fisher, Michael Foster, Terry Healy, Kimberly Minafo, Linda Rudlaff, Danny Trout
Copy Editors: Sylvan Allen, Gina Farago, Karen Brewer Grossman, Karen L. Huffman, Amy Kirtley-Hill, Debbie Shoffner
Cover Artists: Nick Greenwood, Clevell Harris
Art Coordinator: Barry Slate
Artists: Pam Crane, Theresa Lewis Goode, Nick Greenwood, Clevell Harris, Sheila Krill, Clint Moore, Greg D. Rieves, Rebecca Saunders, Barry Slate, Donna K. Teal
Typesetters: Lynette Dickerson, Mark Rainey

President, The Mailbox Book Company™: Joseph C. Bucci
Director of Book Planning and Development: Chris Poindexter
Book Development Managers: Stephen Levy, Elizabeth H. Lindsay, Thad McLaurin, Susan Walker
Curriculum Director: Karen P. Shelton
Traffic Manager: Lisa K. Pitts
Librarian: Dorothy C. McKinney
Editorial and Freelance Management: Karen A. Brudnak
Editorial Training: Irving P. Crump
Editorial Assistants: Terrie Head, Hope Rodgers, Jan E. Witcher